THE GAME

ALSO BY ROBERT BENSON

Between the Dreaming and the Coming True

Living Prayer

Venite: A Book of Daily Prayer

THE GAME

ONE MAN, NINE INNINGS,
A LOVE AFFAIR WITH BASEBALL

ROBERT BENSON

JEREMY P. TARCHER/PENGUIN
a member of
Penguin Group (USA) Inc.
New York

Most Tarcher/Penguin books are available at special quantity discounts for bulk purchase for sales promotions, premiums, fundraising, and educational needs. Special books or book excerpts can be created to fit specific needs. For details, write Penguin Group (USA) Inc. Special Markets, 375 Hudson Street, New York, NY 10014.

Jeremy P. Tarcher/Penguin
a member of
Penguin Group (USA) Inc.
375 Hudson Street
New York, NY 10014
www.penguin.com

First trade paperback edition 2004

The Library of Congress catalogued
the hardcover edition as follows:

Benson, R. (Robert), date.
The game : one man, nine innings,
a love affair with baseball/Robert Benson.
p.   cm.
ISBN 1-58542-101-4
1. Baseball—United States.   I. Title.
GV863.A1 B45   2001   00-054377
796.357—dc21

ISBN 1-58542-341-6 (paperback edition)

Printed in the United States of America
1   3   5   7   9   10   8   6   4   2

BOOK DESIGN BY AMANDA DEWEY

THIS BOOK IS FOR THE HOME TEAM.

Baseball is about homecoming. It is a journey by theft and strength, guile and speed, out around first to the far island of second, where foes lurk in the reefs and the green sea suddenly grows deeper, then to turn sharply, skimming the shallows, making for a shore that will show a friendly face, a color, a familiar language and, at third, to proceed, no longer by paths indirect but straight, to home.

A. BARTLETT GIAMATTI
from *The Hartford Courant*

CONTENTS

A Ceremonial
First Pitch

ANYONE WHO WORKS on books all the time, as opposed to actually doing something useful with their life, has to start somewhere each time that they start a book. Most of us have a way—a habit, a discipline, a ritual, a routine, a nightmare, or something—that is the way that we begin to work on a work.

For me, the work usually grows out of the things that I am reading and studying and learning. I start to make notes about those things in my journal, and I find myself having conversations about those things with my friends, and then it seems that everything that I read and hear and observe and wonder about is pointing at the same thing. Then somewhere along the way, the thing begins to have a shape of some sort, and I start to discover what it is that I am writing.

This book is different. I did not find myself suddenly thinking about baseball, and then writing about it. The truth is that

I am almost always thinking about baseball in a way. "People ask me what I do in winter when there's no baseball," said the great Rogers Hornsby. "I'll tell you what I do. I stare out the window and wait for spring." He spoke for a lot of people, including me.

At almost any point in time, if I had my choice, I would be at the ballpark. I would be in Wrigley Field or Yankee Stadium watching the big leaguers. Or I would be at the ballpark not too far from my house watching the local minor league team. Or I would be over at the school yard watching my children play. Better yet, I would be throwing batting practice to them and their schoolmates and hitting grounders and taking throws.

Whenever you run into me, wherever it is that we are, and whatever it is that we are supposed to be doing, it is wise to remember that I would generally rather be at the ballpark. You would be welcome to come with me, of course. If you plan to come and see me, then bring a glove, because we are going to throw a few before the day is over. "No matter what I talk about, I always get back to baseball," said Connie Mack, the legendary baseball man. It happens to me a lot as well.

Two of my friends came to me last year and asked me if I would like to write a book about baseball. More specifically, they asked if I would like to write a book about the mysticism and the spirituality of baseball. I am not completely certain even now that I completely understand what they meant by that. But I understood something about why they asked me: I write about spiritual things in general and they know that I love baseball. There is a bit of logic to that. I was not about to look askance at such a gift. If someone tells you to take your base, you take your base.

IF ONE IS LOOKING FOR NON-BASEBALL PEOPLE TO
write a book about baseball, one could find plenty of people who
know more about it than I do. In my own small circle of friends,
there are several people who are better candidates for such work.

I know a woman who was in the stadium the day that Bobby
Thomson hit the home run to win the 1951 pennant for the New
York Giants and break the hearts of Brooklyn Dodger fans. I have
a friend who has long had season tickets at Yankee Stadium. I
have another friend who played the game at the minor league
level and almost made it to the show. And one who coaches the
game, and one who has reported on it for the newspapers, and
one who used to work for the Seattle Mariners. I have another
friend who watches every Alanta Braves game on television, tap-
ing them when he has to be on the road the way some people tape
soap operas. I even know a guy who is the chaplain for the New
York Yankees.

Any one of these people knows more about the game than I
do. The difference is that nobody chose them to write a book;
they chose me. So I said yes very quickly. I was afraid the offer
might be withdrawn if I hesitated.

My best credential is that I have season tickets to a Triple-A
park. One of the games played there, a game between the Iowa
Cubs and the Nashville Sounds, is the game that provides a cen-
tral thread for the book. It was an ordinary weeknight game in
the early part of the season between two teams that ended up far
out of first place in the Pacific Coast League. Nothing major happened at all; it was just baseball, and that was enough for me.

WRITERS NEVER REALLY KNOW WHY THEY ARE CHO-
sen to be writers, of course, and neither do I. I just was.

I was chosen long ago to try to write sentences. To be more precise, the thing chose me. "You spend a good piece of your life gripping a baseball," wrote Jim Bouton, "and in the end it turns out that it was the other way around all the time." Writing has been, and still is, exactly that way for me.

It turns out that a fresh bottle of ink, a hunger for word and story and memory, a long and deep love for the game, and, of course, a lucky bounce somehow qualified me to write this book.

At least, that is what got me to be sitting here, pen in hand, assigned to write a book about baseball, to tell some stories about the game I love best, with no rule other than that I am supposed to give it to the people who asked me to write it when I am finished, and along the way to try to say what I have learned from the most mystical and magical and mysterious game of all.

I feel like I just stole home.

R. Benson
Opening Day, 2001

WANT TO GO TO THE GAME?

Much of what we love later in a sport is what it recalls to us about ourselves at our earliest. And those memories, now smoothed and bending away from us in the interior of ourselves, are not simply of childhood or of a childhood game. They are memories of our best hopes. They are memories of a time when all that would be better was before us, as a hope, and the hope was fastened to a game. One hoped not so much to be the best who ever played as simply to stay in the game and ride it wherever it would go, culling its rhythms and realizing its promises. That is, I think, what it means to remember one's best hopes, and to remember them in a game, and revive them whenever one sees the game played, long after playing is over.

A. BARTLETT GIAMATTI
from *The Hartford Courant*

April 18, 2000: Nashville Sounds (the AAA affiliate of the Pittsburgh Pirates) vs. the Iowa Cubs (the AAA affiliate of the Chicago Cubs). Game number 13 for the Sounds, game number 13 for the Cubs. First game of a four-game series. Greer Stadium, Nashville, 6:05 game time. Temperature at game time is 76 degrees. Sky is clear, winds are light and variable.

Starting lineup

IOWA CUBS		NASHVILLE SOUNDS	
2B	Myers	CF	Redman
SS	Ojeda	SS	Nunez
RF	Gonzalez	2B	Wehner
LF	Hatcher	1B	Cruz
1B	Zaleta	C	Laker
CF	Mathews	RF	Brown
3B	Johns	LF	Brede
C	Encarnacion	3B	Patterson
P	Norton	P	Baptist
MGR	D. Trembley	MGR	T. Jewett

It is late on a September Sunday morning and we are in a big Chicago hotel that looks down over the river at about the exact spot where the river meets Lake Michigan.

We are finishing our coffee and our newspapers. It is not a real Sunday to us without the *New York Times,* and this day we get a bonus because we have the *Chicago Tribune* delivered to our door as well. We are trying to figure out the best way to spend the free day that we have managed to pick up in our favorite city. There is an exhibit opening that we both want to see, down at the Art Institute. There is, of course, the pull of the Miracle Mile—it seems there is always something that you *need* there. The best brunch in the city, in our opinion, is just a few blocks down from us, and there is a big festival in Grant Park that will offer up good food and above-average people-watching.

There is a running joke at our house that from April until October we plan all of our business travel around the likelihood of catching a baseball game when we are on the road. We prefer major league games, but we like the minor leagues as well. We live in a minor league city, or rather, as the local civic leaders prefer to say, in a city that has a minor league team.

It does not always work out that we can catch a game, but when someone calls to see if we can be in a certain city at a certain time, one of the first things we do is check and see if the home team is going to be in town or not. If not, it does not mean that we will not make the trip, but if they are in town then it often means that we will go in a day early or stay a day later so that we can catch a game or two before we have to go home. There is absolutely no truth to the rumor that I charge higher fees if the home team is out of town.

I am on a modified Harry Caray plan. "Now, you tell me," said the legendary radio broadcaster to a reporter once, "if I have a day off during the baseball season, where do you think I will spend it? The ball park." I try to never miss a chance to go to one myself, day off or not.

Sometimes I go to watch my children play, or better yet, to play with them. They both like to play the game, and I like to pretend that I can still play it too. All of us like to spend a few hours pretending that we are major leaguers and that we have nothing else to worry about except our footwork or our swing or our arm speed.

Sometimes I go to the minor league park in our town and sometimes to the minor league park in someone else's town. Best of all, of course, is to be able to visit one of the cathedrals of the game—Fenway Park or Yankee Stadium or Camden Yards. My favorite place of all is Wrigley Field in Chicago.

In the end, on that September Sunday morning, the choice is easy. There is a day game at Wrigley, Sammy Sosa is hitting home runs almost as often as is Mark McGwire—it is that record-breaking summer—and we do not have to catch our plane until eight o'clock in the evening. Art exhibits and brunch and all the rest can be done in the winter while we are waiting for the season to begin again.

"Want to go to the game?" says one of us. And the other one grins and heads for the suitcase to pull out the baseball caps and the score books that we brought along just in case.

I HAVE LIVED IN A MAJOR LEAGUE CITY ONLY ONCE, and then only for about two years. I lived in Chicago, which is where I learned to take the train to work and so forth in the city. Which is how I learned that the best way to travel to a baseball game is on the train. To be sure, any method of transport that will get you to a game is a good way to travel, but if you get to choose, take the train.

Half the fun of taking the train to the game is watching the people, which is all the fun of taking the train most of the time. It is also the easiest train trip for a visitor to make in a big city because it is the one train trip you can take in which you hardly ever get lost—you just follow the crowd in the baseball caps, the people who are all geared up as though they are going on safari. They have sunglasses, binoculars, scorecards, hats, banners to wave, signs to hold up, baseball gloves for catching foul balls and home runs, and umbrellas and rain gear no matter what the forecast is. (The only sure way to prevent a rainout is for more than half the crowd to be prepared for the rain to come.) Or you can just get in behind the Little Leaguers wearing their uniforms, or behind the guys in suits and ties and baseball hats, the ones with their jackets off and their shirtsleeves rolled up.

In most cities, the train will be underground for a while, and then it will come out and up onto the elevated tracks and the crowd will all be looking out the windows on the same side of the train. Except for the ones who are not going to the game, who just stare at the floor or scan their newspapers, or take naps, disconsolate and envious, I expect. Unless it is even worse, and they are not baseball fans, and therefore do not even know what they are missing.

The collective heartbeat in the train will go up and up the closer you get to the station for the ballpark. When the stadium comes into view, little ones will shout, "I see it, I see it!" in the way that they do after they get their first glimpse of the ocean after riding in a car all night to get to the beach. Some of the grown-ups will shout too, and not just us out-of-towners.

ONE DOES NOT TAKE THE TRAIN TO GREER STADIUM in Nashville. One does not take the train anywhere in Nashville; we are a car town, not a train town. There used to be trolleys here, years ago, and there are plenty of tracks around, including some just behind the left-field wall at Greer, but there are no passenger trains of any sort.

Greer Stadium is the home of the Nashville Sounds, one of the farm teams for the Pittsburgh Pirates. The Sounds play in the Pacific Coast League, an odd fact that must make sense to somebody, somewhere. We are a few miles from the Pacific Ocean, to say the least.

Greer is almost thirty years old. It was built to house a Single-A franchise years ago, and I read somewhere that if it were being built today it would never pass the codes and guidelines for a Triple-A park, which is what it is now. I have a sense that when it was built back in the seventies, the owners thought that the stadium would not be here very long. They were dreaming and planning and hoping to land a major league expansion franchise, and I think they assumed that the stadium they were building would soon be torn down to make room for a major league park. It never happened. We fans of baseball in Nashville have learned to find meaning in our lives in other ways, though it is a struggle.

It is not a pretty ballpark architecturally, not like the old ones that are still around from the thirties and forties. It is not even like the new ones that are being built here and there with a kind of retro look—Camden Yards in Baltimore, or Coors Field in Denver, or the new home of the minor league Memphis Redbirds, the one that just opened this year in Memphis right across the street from the Peabody Hotel and a few blocks from the Mississippi River and a block or two from Beale Street.

Greer Stadium was built near the site of an old ballpark in Nashville that was torn down years ago. At one time the old park was the home of a Negro League franchise. Later it was the home of the old Nashville Vols, the minor league team that my father used to go to see when he was young. The ballpark was known then as Fort Negley, and it was called that because there used to be a Federal fort here during the Civil War. You can still see some of the stone walls that go back up into the hill where the fort used to be. If you sit on the stone walls, you can look down over the parking lot toward the stadium, and you can see the top of the scoreboard and watch pop flies go up in the air during batting practice. My son reminded me the other day that we had a picnic there on those stone walls the first time that he ever came to the ballpark. I had forgotten that, and I wonder now if my father ever sat on one of those walls when he was young.

Greer has been the home of minor league franchises for the Reds, the Yankees, the Tigers, the White Sox, and now for the Pirates. So there are some big-league players that have come through here on their way up or their way back down, as well as some who dropped by for a week of rehab or some such thing. Don Mattingly and Steve Balboni and Paul O'Neill played here. As did Barry Larkin and Pete Rose, Jr. and Rob Dibble of the Reds. And Willie McGee and Otis Nixon and Tim Raines and Keith Lockhart. When we watch a game on television, we almost always see someone who has played here.

Going to see a game at Greer is not like going to Wrigley or some of the other places that one might go. But when I am in Row 6, Section J, four rows behind the dugout on the first-base side, it is the prettiest ballpark in the world. Because it is the one where I have season tickets, and therefore it is the one I get to go to forty or fifty times a year.

THE WEATHER IN CHICAGO ON OUR STOLEN SUNDAY is brisk. It is September, and though fall is not yet here, there is an edge to the breeze. The air is clean, though the sky is growing gray. The season will be over soon, and when it is, summer will be gone too.

We take a cab to the subway stop, because we have waited until it is almost too late to go. But once we have decided to go to the game, there is no turning back. And the sooner we get there, the better, because the game is sold out, and we still have to find tickets on the street.

Down into the subway station at State and Lake we go, cold air from deep within the city blowing up into our faces. (Because it is Sunday, there are not many people underground, not like there are on workdays.) Then we are rolling under the river in the dark and headed north. We come back out into the light on the near north side, then fly along above the neighborhoods down below. Along with everyone else on the train, we are watching for the flags that will tell us that we are nearing the stadium. When you get close enough to Wrigley Field to see the flags high above the brick walls, you know that you are close to heaven.

When you get close to Greer Stadium, there are not many flags. But you can see the one-hundred-and-fifteen-foot guitar.

THE SCOREBOARD AT GREER STADIUM IS BUILT IN the shape of a guitar. A giant guitar for a scoreboard is one of those things that happen from time to time when one lives in a place that is known as Music City, U.S.A.

From time to time, I will buy a book about making trips to minor league ballparks around the country, and there is always an entry for Nashville. There is always a picture of the 115-foot guitar-shaped scoreboard in the book, as though seeing the world's largest scorekeeping guitar might be a good reason to visit Nashville. It may be, I do not know. If it was in Birmingham, I am not sure that I would make the drive, but it is hard to say. I live in a town that has a scorekeeping guitar, and so I am unsure about what life is like without one. It could be something that it is worth the drive to see.

Some folks that I know here in town are very sentimental about the scoreboard, the same way that many people are about the hand-operated one that can still be found at Fenway Park in Boston. I do not really feel that way about the big guitar, especially since it no longer explodes with fireworks when the home team hits a home run the way that it used to. But sometimes there is talk about building a new ballpark here, and even I must admit that if they build a new park and do not keep the old guitar, something will have been lost.

Except for the fact that it has frets and keys and such, it looks and operates pretty much like any other scoreboard. It is also the way that huge home runs are measured here. In Chicago, they talk about the ones that were hit out of the park and into Waveland Avenue, one of the streets that run alongside Wrigley Field. In Nashville, the really big home runs are the ones that go over the guitar. In the ballpark where I grew up, or tried to, the really big ones were the ones that went all the way to the trees.

WHEN I WAS YOUNG, WE USED TO PRACTICE AND play our baseball at Drakes Creek Park.

It was maybe forty or fifty acres of land that was bound by a four-lane highway to the west and by the lake to the south. Drakes Creek is actually the name of a long finger of the big lake that had flooded in when the TVA built a dam on the Cumberland River. The eastern border of the park was a grove of old trees that marked the edge of a suburban neighborhood, and the first of those trees was the tree that separated the average home runs from the monster home runs. There were home runs, and then there were home runs that went past the tree.

Up a gentle hill about three hundred yards or so behind one of the two baseball diamonds, to the north, was Cherokee Road. If you took Cherokee Road about two miles east from there, following its winding way along Drakes Creek, you would intersect with Indian Lake Road, which then wandered around through fields for three miles or so and delivered you unto our house. We did not live at the end of the line, but you could see it from there.

Most days, most of the year, we would take Indian Lake Road from our house straight out to the highway because it was quicker. Two months a year we took Cherokee Road to the highway because it was baseball season. From about the middle of June to the middle of August, Drakes Creek Park was the center of the universe, and Coach Taylor was its king and prophet and guru and pied piper.

During the school year, Coach Taylor was a history teacher and the varsity basketball coach at the high school. He was a small, energetic man, left-handed as I recall, with a permanent suntan and a black crew cut. There was more than a little bit of drill instructor about him. I was invited to practice with the high school basketball team when I was in junior high school, when he was still the basketball coach. He said that I did not have much talent but that I had quickness and brains and that he could turn me into a point guard if I would let him. It turned out that first he had to try to kill me with running drills.

He was not a local boy; he was from up on the Cumberland Plateau, which is eighty or ninety miles east of us, and he had been an athlete at a small college up there somewhere. He was one of the thousands of small-town boys who played ball growing up and then somehow decided that they could think of no finer way to spend a life than to be around games and the kids who played them. If you had to teach history to do it, or make a small salary all your life, or put up with moms and dads who were not happy when their kids did not get to play enough, then so be it. The relief pitcher Bill Lee, of the Boston Red Sox, when asked if being a relief pitcher was hard, once said: "It beats lifting stuff." Coach Taylor must have thought something like that about being a coach.

In the summer, Coach Taylor ran the baseball camp and the Little League. I did not know it then, but teachers had to do something to make a living in the summer, as though what they did during the other nine months was not worth a year's pay. I suspect he coached baseball because he needed the money. But for those eight or ten weeks, when some eighty to one hundred kids would show up and put themselves in his hands, if he did not love the game and the teaching of it, I could not tell it.

Every day in those summers, my mother or my father would drop my brother and me off along the edge of the park up on Cherokee Road. We would have our practice clothes on, and our team hats, with the bill of the hat folded just right so that it would fit in your pocket when you were in the dugout or at bat. (Look at a picture of Mickey Mantle in his hat and you can see the proper way to fold it.) Over one shoulder we had our bat with our glove hanging off it. Over the other shoulder we carried a bag with everything needed for a perfect summer day: bubble gum, a clean uniform for the game in the evening, a bathing suit and towel, a peanut butter sandwich and a bag of chips in a brown paper sack, a little money for hot dogs at the concession stand or a walk to the Dairy Queen between games, and a pair of tennis shoes that our mother made us carry in case we had to take our spikes off, which we never did if we could help it.

We would head down the hill for the concession stand first, a little cinder-block building that stood in the middle of the park underneath the big oak tree that we all huddled under if the rain came. The tree was better shelter than the dugouts. It was the same oak tree under which we were supposed to meet our parents when it was time to go home.

Coach Taylor would drive up in his old pickup truck, unlock the door at the back of the concession stand, and start handing things out to us. There would be bases for the two fields; a bag of batting helmets for each dugout; buckets of baseballs, one for the outfield, one for home plate, one for second base, one for the pitcher's mound; a bag of bats for each dugout; and sometimes a half-dozen rakes to be pushed and dragged around until the infields were smoothed out from the games that had been played the night before.

For a while we would make like a grounds crew, hauling equipment for a while and raking the infield for a while and picking up trash for a while. Sometimes one or another of us had to cut grass or shovel dirt into the holes left by catchers and hitters and plate umpires. You did not have to work if you did not want to, but we could not take the field until the work was done. Besides, Coach Taylor liked guys who worked hard, and you wanted him to like you.

When the fields were ready, we would start to be ballplayers. We would run the outfield to loosen up, and then sit in a circle to stretch. We would throw back and forth with someone to get our arms loose, ten feet apart at first, then thirty feet, then sixty, then ninety. Then we would head off to our positions and smooth out the dirt around it with our feet and toss pebbles over the lines and into the grass in foul territory, while chewing our gum and blowing bubbles and holding our gloves on our hips the way our major league heroes did. The outfielders would throw pop flies to each other and the infielders would pick up the grounders rolled to them by the first basemen and fire the balls back across the diamond.

After a while Coach Taylor would come to the plate with a bat and we would start to take infield, taking grounders and making throws and working on our footwork. He taught us to charge a ground ball so it would not eat you up and get past you, and to make throws that would be chest-high every time. The outfielders learned to run down fly balls, and worked on throwing the ball on a line so that it would hop cleanly enough to be caught by an infielder in a position to tag the runner. The pitchers would go off to the side to practice the black arts that, in the evening when the games were actually played, would make them the stars of their teams and the spoilers of dreams. All of the players on all of the teams worked out together in the mornings; there were no enemies until the evening.

By nine o'clock we were hot and sweaty, by ten o'clock we were already better than we were the day before, and by eleven o'clock we were dreaming of playing in the big leagues. By noon we were standing in line like a bunch of kids again, getting ready to walk the two miles to Smith's Pool.

———

THERE WILL BE MORE THAN FORTY THOUSAND FANS in Wrigley Field before the day is through, crammed into every crook and cranny of what is known as the "friendly confines." So, when we get off the train at Wrigley Field in Chicago, the line into the stadium starts at the steps that lead down from the elevated train platform. And we are pretty much in line for about three blocks after that.

The line goes down the steps and through the turnstiles. Then left through the station house and right through the doors— shuffle-step, "excuse me," bump, "sorry," shuffle-step, "hold my hand," you say to your companion if you are not alone. When you come out the door you are on Addison Street and headed west, and you come out into what is, most days at least, a city street in an old neighborhood. On game days, you come out into a sort of family reunion that is populated by people that you somehow know but do not recognize, and you are surrounded by a strange and wondrous sort of street fair.

There are lines everywhere. There are lines along the sidewalk and in front of the ATM. There are lines of vendors hawking game-day souvenirs, and lines of cars trying to squeeze into parking lots, and lines of customers four-deep in the bars along the block, and lines of people at the ticket windows and the turnstiles.

We follow the line down the steps to the street, and our first stop is the pub at the corner, where one of us can order some lunch while the other one seeks out tickets. The bartender checks the room for me, looking for anyone who has good tickets to sell, but comes up empty. I go out to the corner and start to walk the blocks around the stadium slowly, two fingers in the air. After a while, after a half-dozen passes by the same vendor selling hats, he nods his head. Evidently some days I look more like an under-cover cop than I know, and on this day it took a few passes for him to recognize me as a pilgrim and produce two box seats at face value.

The gates will open soon; the lines are already passing through the turnstiles.

THERE ARE LINES AT GREER STADIUM FROM TIME to time, though nothing like those you find at Wrigley or any other major league park, of course.

The longest lines here generally form on Wednesdays during the summer. The club offers some sort of promotional ticket package to most of the day camps and other summer programs for kids in the area. And on Wednesdays, they have games that start at noon so that those kids can come. Sometimes you forget about it until you pull into the driveway and go around behind the stadium to the parking lot and see the lines of buses along the fence that stretches back up the hill away from the rear entrance. And there are long lines of kids, all in their camp T-shirts, with their ball caps on their heads and their baseball gloves hanging off their hands. They use their other hand to hold hands with their buddy so that they can get lost together. At the front of the line, and sort of interspersed at intervals along the line, there are pairs of adults who have come as chaperones and crossing guards and mediators and dispensers of hot-dog money. They have cameras and tote bags and water bottles and sunscreen and comfortable shoes and little bunches of tickets that they hand out, one to each kid, so that each kid can hand a ticket to Mr. Jack at the gate. After that, the kids disperse throughout the ballpark, each of them watching roughly an inning and a half of baseball all told, and spending seven and a half innings watching the back of someone's head while standing in line at the concession stands. They are purists; they are in this for the cotton candy, which is as it should be.

THE LINE WE LITTLE LEAGUERS WALKED IN OVER TO Smith's Pool must have stretched out about forty or fifty yards. Coach Taylor led it, of course, marching steadily along, turning back from time to time to see that we were all still with him, occasionally turning back to cajole or encourage or tell a joke or speak to one of us about something that happened on the field that morning.

We walked in pairs along the side of Saunders Ferry Road, along the shoulder past the little bait shop, the market, and the firehouse, and then along the edge of the lake. If you slipped there you could drop a few feet into the mud along the shore. Later, on the way back, we would curve past the street where I used to live, the one that ran about six blocks to the old elementary school, and then we would go past the Sinclair station where Mr. Rhoades would look up from pumping gas or come out from behind his gray metal desk and say hello as we went by.

We spent the late afternoons lazing around the ballpark, throwing a little, and hitting sometimes. Then we would help line the baselines and brush off the bases and rake the infields again. Folks, including our own, would start to turn up, the lines of cars coming into the park to pull up in the grass. We would change into our uniforms and wander around until the coach for the team that we played on had arrived, and then we would sit in circles in the grass while the coaches tried to be Casey Stengel. But we had already been ballplayers all day and needed little or no instruction from a man who had spent the day in a tie and a suit and an office.

EVERY TIME I STAND IN LINE AT A BALLPARK, I AM aware of the people who have stood in such a line before, and of the people who are somehow still standing beside me. There are my childhood friends Ricky and Nicky and the rest, and my brother and my dad. Coach Taylor, who taught me how to play in the days when I thought I would be the next great Yankee infielder. I think of lying on my back on the hook rug in my grandfather's living room watching the Game of the Week on black-and-white television and learning to say "Podna" with Dizzy Dean and Pee Wee Reese. I remember watching the World Series on television at school, back in the days when the Series was played in the sunlight and the teachers were following it as well. I remember the stickball games played with broomsticks and tennis balls, the ones that we used to play on camping trips with families whose fathers were named Henry and Billy and Joe.

The lines always remind me of Paul, who follows the Braves, and Lori, who pulls for the Mariners. They remind me of the day that the Chicago Cubs missed the World Series by a couple of innings, the day I watched the game on television in Nashville while my best friend watched it five hundred miles away in Chicago. We lost a chance to see the Cubs go to the Series and ran up a three-hour long-distance bill at the same time.

I remember arriving before batting practice began and stand-

ing in the line at the gates to get into Coors Field in Denver on a
hot summer afternoon the year that the ballpark opened. And I
remember the long line of cars trying to get into the parking lots
of Camden Yards in Baltimore and Dodger Stadium in Los Angeles. I remember the line of Yankee fans on the steps coming
down from the elevated train in the Bronx, and the long line of
people that stretched out along the sidewalks that run down the
hill to Turner Field in Atlanta.

Every line is different and every line is the same.

WHEN MY MOTHER WOULD LET US OUT AT THE BALL-
park on those summer mornings, she would let us out up on
Cherokee Road. And we would walk down the hill to the ballpark.

I wish that I had paid more attention when I got out of the car
those days. But I do think I have one pretty clear memory of sort
of pausing at the top of the hill one day, waving good-bye to
Mother, putting my bag over my shoulder, and looking down
the slope the hundred yards or so to the diamonds below. The
memory seems clear, but it may just be that I wish that I could
still see it.

Sometimes we were the first ones there, but not very often.
Sometimes we missed the grounds-crew part. Being the first to
arrive was not one of the characteristics of the family that I grew
up in. Almost always there were guys there ahead of us. And as we
walked down the hill, our steps would start getting faster as we
drew closer.

The sounds of the ballpark must have floated up to us as we
walked—the sound of the bat on the ball, the ball in the glove.

The sound of spikes in the dirt, and the whistle of some infielder calling for the ball, and the crash of a ball into the screen behind the plate. The sound of youthful voices, calling out the chatter in the infield. "The only perfect pleasure we ever knew," Clarence Darrow called it.

The colors must have come up at us too. The shades of white in the uniforms and the baseballs and the bases and the lines. The green of the grass and the red of the infield dirt. The blues and reds and oranges and greens of ball caps and the golden dust that got kicked up as players moved back and forth.

One can smell a ballpark. The grass, the breeze, and the dirt all mingle together with the smell of the water used to knock the dust down in the infield and around the plate. There is the damp, cool smell of the dugout and the sharp scent of leather and wood and sweat and dirt. It would be foolish of me to say that I noticed all these things when I was young, but I do remember them now that I am older.

"Every player should be accorded the privilege of playing at least one season with the Chicago Cubs," said Alvin Dark once, a man who did so for a few seasons before he went on to manage the San Francisco Giants. "That's baseball as it should be played— in God's own sunshine."

That is why most all of us who love the game love Wrigley Field. When you come into the stadium on the field level, and you head down toward your seat, the park is so small and the seats so near the field that you can see and hear and smell everything in every ballpark that ever was. If I stop for a moment, trying to take it all in slowly, which I always try to do now, I am somehow transported back across time to those summer days when I would make my way to the ballpark by coming down the hill from Cherokee Road. I can close my eyes and listen carefully and breathe deeply and all of those summer days come back to me. I can see me and my brother and my friends. I can hear my dad cheering and the crowd talking. I can hear Coach Taylor shouting out "Get one and cover" while we take infield, and the chatter as we fire it around the horn.

For a little while, nine innings at least, I am home again.

MAY I HAVE THIS DANCE?

The game begins in the spring, when everything else begins again, and it blossoms in the summer, filling the afternoons and evenings, and then as soon as the chill rains come, it stops and leaves you to face the fall alone. You count on it, rely on it to buffer the passage of time, to keep the memory of sunshine and high skies alive, and then just when the days are all twilight, when you need it most, it stops.

A. BARTLETT GIAMATTI
The Yale Alumni Magazine

CUBS 1ST *(Sounds 0, Cubs 0)—Myers grounds out to Nunez at shortstop. Ojeda flies out to Redman in center field. Gonzalez flies to Brown in right. (0 runs, 0 hits, 0 errors, 0 left on base)*

SOUNDS 1ST *(Sounds 0, Cubs 0)—Redman grounds out to Johns at third. Nunez walks. Wehner walks, moving Nunez to second. Cruz grounds to Myers at second, who forces Wehner at second base; Cruz reaches on the fielder's choice and Nunez advances to third. Laker singles to center, scoring Nunez and advancing Cruz to second. Brown strikes out looking for the third out. (1 run, 1 hit, 0 errors, 2 LOB)*

IN MOST OF THE COUNTRY
the weather is still too cold for baseball when baseball begins
every year at spring training, and the weather is generally too cold
for baseball when the season ends with the World Series in October. In between, the game is generally played in warm weather if
not downright hot weather. It is the game of summer, and we are
so anxious for summer after winter that we push the season a bit.
It is cool and pleasant at Greer on this spring night only twelve
days past Opening Day. The temperature has been in the low seventies most all day, and even though it will get cool when the sun
goes all the way down, it will be a good night for a game.

In the way that early-spring afternoons are, it is breezy and
warm for a few minutes, blustery and cool for a few minutes, still
and hot for a few minutes after that. I am reasonably certain that
I am going to spend most of the evening juggling my way in and
out of my jacket, while trying to hold my scorecard and my pen-

cils, my hot dogs and my beer, and trying to keep an eye on the game at the same time.

Walking through the concourse, my teeth wanting to chatter from the wind that is whipping down under the stadium—the winter's reflexes are still with me—I can hear the crack of a bat on a baseball. The sound is always different in the early days of April than it is in the humidity and heat of July. The sound of it today is like the sound of the bat at the very beginning of the season, when it is rainy and cold and when summer and baseball are somewhere between a memory and a hope. The season does not begin when warm weather arrives.

Everything begins long before that.

LAST YEAR THE SEASON BEGAN FOR US IN BETWEEN basketball games on a cold, misty Saturday afternoon in late February. We even had a snow flurry or two that day.

My daughter's team had won their game in the morning, largely due to her good rebounding and putback baskets—her father's coaching had some small part to play in that, he said humbly. That qualified them to play for the championship in the afternoon, and left us with about four hours to kill in the suburbs, and we were twenty-five miles from home. It was too short a time to go home, and too long a time to hang around the gym.

We were not sure what to do with the time, and so we did what one is supposed to do at such moments: We found a place to eat. She ordered the food and I went out and found the newspapers. As we finished up the french fries, I just happened to call her attention to an article in the sports pages about the fact that spring training was starting that week. Her eyes lit up just as I thought they might. At heart she is a ballplayer, not a re-bounder.

We talked for a few minutes about pitchers and catchers reporting early, and then about who had been traded in the off-season and who had retired and who had joined our favorite teams. We talked about the World Series just past and about her school softball season to come. We also talked about how unfair it was that Arizona and Florida got to have spring training every year, and then had been awarded three expansion franchises between them as well. We were unsure as to whether we should appeal to the major league office or the Supreme Court or the United Nations, but we were, and still are, certain that we have a grievance.

Then I just happened to remember that I had put a bag of balls in the trunk of the car that morning when we left for the basketball game, and she grinned. As luck would have it, I had thrown our spikes and gloves and bats and warm-up jackets in too. That, too, seemed to please her somehow. Being a father is a little like being a hitter sometimes: It is a guessing game, and on this particular day, at this particular at-bat, I had guessed correctly.

Ten minutes later, she was running down fly balls in center field at the ball park behind the school where the basketball tournament was being held, her long legs gliding across the wet grass, the wind whipping her blond ponytail around, her steps sure and graceful.

She and I were the only ones outside at the park, and there was no sound but the sound of the bat on the ball and then the sound of the ball hitting leather as she hauled it in. "That's the true harbinger of spring," noted Bill Veeck, the legendary Chicago baseball man, "not crocuses or swallows returning to Capistrano, but the sound of the bat on the ball."

It is the happiest sound of the spring, and maybe even the happiest sound of the whole year. It means that summer and sunshine and baseball are just around the corner. And hearing it while snow flurries fall around you gently does nothing to make it any less sweet.

SOME OF THE PEOPLE WHO CLAIM THAT THEY DO NOT like baseball say that it is because everything about baseball is too long. The season goes on too long in the first place, they say, and a game does too. It has no clock, it can go on for hours without anyone scoring a run, even an inning can seem like it lasts for days sometimes.

According to Ray Fitzgerald, a writer for *The Boston Globe,* "A critic once characterized baseball as six minutes of action crammed into two and one-half hours." My friends who love basketball and football more than baseball are generally quick to point out something like this when I ask them to go to the game with me. My general recommendation to them is that they go to the ballpark two hours earlier. They are not seeing too much of the game, they are seeing too little.

Ballparks open two hours before game time, and when you go through the gate and enter the stadium, there is a dance taking place that you need to see. The dance is virtually the same no matter who is playing or what ballpark you are in. There are some variations from team to team, and some variations from day to day for particular players, but it is pretty much the same everywhere from college on up. The dance is known as batting practice.

It is a little like going into any Catholic or Anglican church in the world on a Sunday morning. No matter where I travel or what city or town that I find myself in, if I go into one of those places, I am instantly a participant because the dance of the liturgy is the same in all of those places. With some minor variations—the size of the choir, the number of the anthems, the caliber of the homily—the dance is the same one that they are practicing in my hometown that morning in the place where I would be if I were there. I am at home in any of those places because I have learned to see and watch and love the dance itself.

If you arrive in time for batting practice, you sit in virtually empty seats and watch the dance below on the field. You can move from seat to seat, even section to section if you are there early enough and you are so inclined and you know how to chat up the ushers.

The first thing that you notice about the field is that there is a huge tarpaulin spread out over the dirt around home plate. There is a long canvas runner that goes from home plate to the pitcher's mound, which is also covered by a tarp. They are protecting the dirt around the mound and the plate so that it will be smooth for the game. Sitting on the tarp at home plate is a big cage made of metal pipes and screens. It is like a giant quarter of a ball, set on rollers and then rolled out to cover the area around home plate.

There will be a crowd around the back and sides of the cage, a dozen or so players and coaches and hitting instructors standing in a sort of loose circle. Each batter in turn will take six or eight or ten swings at the plate, and then step out as someone else jumps in. You can see the first batter back outside the cage, practicing his swing in slow motion, trying to work out some little kink in it or commit this swing to muscle memory even more deeply. Sometimes a coach will come over and say something to him, sometimes not. The hitting instructors are watching for little things that can help a hitter or hurt an average. Then the hitter will step back in to take more cuts. Three or four or five turns altogether, thirty or forty pitches, more or less depending on how he is hitting these days or whether he is more likely to play today or to be sitting on the bench or in the bullpen.

It is serious business, this trying to learn to hit a baseball. "The hardest thing to do in baseball is to hit a round baseball with a round bat, squarely," observed Ted Williams, arguably the one who did it better than anyone else. Though it may look like a crowd of boys just taking turns showing each other how far they can hit one, such work can be the difference between staying in the game or being forced to give it up, something none of those boys down there want to do now that they have earned the right to play on the fields of their dreams.

Sometimes I watch the hitters from the stands right behind the cage, so that I can watch the swings and listen to the talk among the players. Sometimes I find myself drawn to the outfield seats for a while because they are the best place to collect souvenir baseballs. The other place I like to go is down by the dugouts, because that is where one can most easily get an autograph or meet a player as he comes in from the field to take his turn at bat. I do not collect autographs seriously, but I do like to listen to the players talk to the people who do.

The man on the mound for all of this is either a left-hander, if the team will be facing a left-handed pitcher today, or a right-hander, if the opposition is starting a right-hander today. He is seldom a pitcher, at least not an active one. More often he is a coach.

Beside him is a shopping cart full of baseballs, and he pulls them out of the cart three or four at a time. He has no glove on his off hand and he is pitching from the front of the mound, rather than on top of it, about eight or ten feet closer to the plate than usual. Being that close to the hitter can get you killed if you are not careful, so there is a screen set up in front of him to protect him from the ball when it is sent back his way, and he just throws pitches in as fast and as hard as he can, in a kind of rhythm that only ballplayers know, with enough time for the hitter to get set, but quickly enough so that everybody can get their work in during the short time allotted to each team.

For an hour, every six or eight seconds, there is a pitch coming to the plate and somebody is trying to hit it squarely, more squarely than he hit it the last time, trying to get it right, again and again.

THE SNOW FLURRIES NOTWITHSTANDING, IT DID NOT take too long for my daughter and me to get into a rhythm ourselves that February afternoon.

I reach into the bucket for a ball, toss it up, and loft a fly to her in center field. This art has a baseball name—hitting fungoes. There is even a special bat made for it, though you do not have to have one of those.

George Plimpton, the writer who has made a life, if not a career, out of trying on various and sundry professional sports uniforms and talking his way into some professional clubhouse and then onto the field to play in an exhibition game or something, once observed that of all his experiences as a "major leaguer," "there was no lazier or more pleasant pastime than watching good fungoes hit, unless it was catching them." Hitting good fungoes has to rank up there somewhere, though, especially when you are hitting them to your child and it is the week of the opening of spring training.

I stand about twenty feet in front of home plate; the point is to get it to her, not to see how far I can hit it. I already know how far I cannot hit it. I watch her for a second or two to see her start back two steps, always the way to start to catch a fly ball, and then I watch her move forward or right or left. When I see that I have actually hit it to her and that she is under it, I bend over to get a ball out of the bucket. As I bend down, I can hear the pop as the ball disappears into her glove. When I straighten up, the first ball is landing softly between second base and the pitcher's mound, where she has been taught to throw it; there is no need to hurt your arm or shoulder while you are practicing your glove work.

The ball rolls past on its way to the backstop. As it passes, I toss the next one up, and here we go again. When the bucket is empty, I drop the bat and head for the screen to pick up the balls and fill up the bucket.

As I bend over to pick up balls, I can hear the sound of singing in center field: "It's the most wonderful time of the year. . . ." Most children sing that song at Christmas; my daughter sings it at the beginning of spring training. "There'll be baseballs for throwing, and bubbles for blowing, so be of good cheer," she sings and laughs. She believes that this is the happiest season of all. I believe, for a moment at least, that I am among the best fathers of all.

DURING A REAL BATTING PRACTICE, THERE ARE PRO-tective screens set up at four or five other places in the infield.

There is a screen behind second base, just on the outfield grass, where balls that are hit to the outfield are thrown back in to someone, usually a batboy, who catches the throws and puts the balls in a bucket. From time to time, the bucket will become full and he will carry it to the mound and pour the balls into the shopping cart.

These balls are being returned to the infield by the crowd of ballplayers that are in the outfield seemingly milling around. They are out near the warning track, spread out in a semicircle made ragged by players bunching up in twos and threes to talk, outfielders and pitchers and bench players, those who are not likely to get into the game at all today, and they are chasing down the balls that come flying out of the cage at home plate. They move slowly and languidly most of the time, gliding across the grass with the grace of the gifted. In the corners of the outfield, there are players throwing or stretching, or a pitcher getting his off-day throwing in, being intently watched by a coach who is looking for the telltale signs that the pitcher's arm is getting better or getting worse.

A third and a fourth screen are at first base and third base respectively, to shield the first baseman and the third baseman from balls being sent through the infield by the guys in the cage. While the hitters are taking their cuts, infielders will be at their positions, taking ground balls and making throws, working on footwork and timing, getting used to the feel of a particular field on a particular day. If you look to the right and left of the plate, about fifteen feet up the lines toward first and toward third, you will see a coach or an instructor or a manager or a pitcher with a day off at each spot, and each one will have a bat in his hands.

They take turns hitting ground balls to the infielders, in the little space in time that is to be found between the crack of the bat in the cage and the next pitch that comes in from the mound.

Everyone is moving all the time, it seems. There are baseballs flying everywhere, and there are little pops of sound from gloves and bats. And there are laughter and shouting here and there. There is rock and roll, too, blasting away over the public-address system.

Every six or eight seconds the steps in the dance begin again. The pitcher throws to home and a ball is cracked out toward the outfield. As it flies through the air, the coach up the first-base line will toss another one up and slap a ground ball toward shortstop. The fly ball from home plate is caught in the outfield about the same time that the shortstop flips the ball to the second baseman to work on his double-play timing.

As the second baseman gloves the ball, the batboy at the screen behind second will haul in the ball being tossed back in from the outfield. The second baseman will wheel and fire the ball to first to complete the imaginary double play as the pitcher throws another one toward the plate, and the hitter swings and sends it screaming toward the outfield wall. The coach on the third-base side smacks a ground ball to second. The first baseman lobs the ball back to the guy hitting fungoes on the first-base side, a high, easy toss that takes one hop so that it can be caught bare-handed by the fungo man. Then the first baseman turns to take the throw from the infielder who has just picked up a ground ball.

This sweet dance is danced by the forty or fifty ballplayers on this great, green dance floor at your feet. It is brand-new today, and it is timeless as well.

This is how the game begins every spring, how it begins every day, and how it began for the Sounds and the Cubs on this April afternoon. It begins this way for a reason.

THE CROWD IS STILL FILING INTO GREER STADIUM as the game gets under way, maybe three thousand of us tonight, maybe less. It is a six o'clock start and school is still in session and there were not many of us here for batting practice.

I wanted to come for batting practice tonight so that I could get a look at the guys who would be playing for us. This was actually my own personal Opening Day this year. The Sounds played their first few games of the season on the road, and then I was on the road for their first few home games, and so I have not really begun the season yet. Tonight they are playing the Iowa Cubs, the Triple-A affiliate of the Chicago Cubs. Even though we are Braves fans and Yankees fans at our house by and large, every baseball fan has a soft spot for anyone who plays in a Cubs uniform, even if it is a minor league Cubs uniform. They usually have some guys that I have seen play at Wrigley or will see there in the summer, and so it is fun for me when they come to town.

It is April, and everyone who roots for any team believes that their team might end up in first place. Iowa Cubs are just as hopeful as Chicago Cubs in April. Pittsburgh players in Pirates uniforms and in Sounds uniforms are hopeful too, and so are their fans. In our hearts we know better, but it is April, the season when all things are possible.

The first batter for the Cubs slaps the ball on about four hops to the shortstop. Nunez gloves it cleanly and guns it to first. Just like batting practice, I think to myself, only without the screens.

Two more hitters, two more swings, two fly balls lifted to the out-field, two more outs. The side is retired and the home team comes to bat. This is why they practice these simple things over and over.

MY DAUGHTER PLAYS FOUR DIFFERENT POSITIONS: shortstop, first base, second base, and center field. So when we work out, doing our own version of the dance, we work some on all four. Once the season starts and her coach has decided where she will play, that is where she will concentrate her work.

"There's no time to think about the right way to make a play and *then* make the play. You just have to do it." So said Bill Free-han in his book. So you work on as many plays as you can, as hard as you know how, over and over again.

I hit twenty ground balls to short and she makes twenty throws to first. When there are only the two of us, she throws to the screen behind first base. We hang a T-shirt up for a target, so she can practice throwing through the imaginary first baseman. You want to learn to throw to the chest every time, and the way to do it is to throw farther than you have to when you practice.

Then she moves to first, where the balls are now scattered along the fence. When you are playing first base and a throw goes bad, you have to turn your back to the infield, run to pick up the ball, and fire it somewhere to keep a runner from advancing on the bad throw. So I put my bat down and pick up my glove and the ball bucket and head for second. She stretches out from first and pretends a throw has gotten by her from some infielder and she runs to the fence to pick up a ball and fire it to second—the throw has to be low so that the runner can be tagged. It takes a lot of pretending to learn to play baseball.

Then I throw the balls to first, pretending to be the shortstop who has just fielded a ground ball, while she practices finding the bag with her feet while keeping her eyes on the ball, and stretching out as far as she can to be sure she gets the imaginary runner. She fires the ball toward home, to another shirt on the fence, to practice cutting down the runner at the plate—the one that took off for home when the shortstop picked up the ground ball. Twenty catches, twenty throws to the plate.

Then she goes back to short and I hit grounders to her that she flips to second to start the double play. We put a bucket about four feet behind second on the right-field side, about where the second baseman would be when cutting across to the bag. If you underhand the ball just right, the ball should hit the bucket every time.

Then I move the bucket of balls to where a second baseman might be if a double play started from the other side. My daughter is at short, in ready position, looking in at the plate. I say go and she moves toward second to take the throw from me and then step on the base, sliding her feet out past the equipment bag we have put down to show where a sliding runner from first base would be. Then she fires the ball to first, to the T-shirt on the fence. Twenty tosses, twenty catches, twenty digs out of the glove while you are moving, twenty slide steps, twenty throws to first.

Then I go to first, because that is where the balls are now, and throw grounders to her at shortstop so that she can practice picking up grounders and firing them to the plate from there. Then I go back to the plate and hit hard smashes through the hole at sec-

ond so that she can work on her range going to her left. The ones
that get through I retrieve in the outfield, and she practices coming out to take relay throws and then firing the ball to the base
that I call out to her while the ball is in the air so she can work on
her footwork and her arm strength.

Then the girl who years ago decided that she wanted to be the
first woman to play for the Yankees takes a break for a minute while
I pick up balls and rearrange the T-shirts and the equipment-bag
markers so that she can work on fielding grounders and line drives
at first. It is uncertain which position the Yankees will be trying to
fill when she is a twenty-two-year-old phenom, and so she is going
to be ready to play at least three positions. The next Derek Jeter
moves from short to first, and as she smooths the dirt around with
her cleats, she thinks about the Braves and about who will replace
Andres Galarraga instead. Someone will someday, and it might as
well be her.

WITH TWO MEN ON IN THE SOUNDS' HALF OF THE
first, our first baseman hits a sharp ground ball to second. Myers,
the Cub second baseman, makes a nice play to keep the ball in the
infield and flips to second to start the double play that will end
the inning. It is hard to know where the split second went—the
throw from Myers to the shortstop, an extra step at the bag by
Ojeda as he came across the bag and forced Wehner out at second, a tick lost as Ojeda took the ball out of his glove before he
threw to first, a throw that was not snapped off quite as cleanly as
it should be—but the split second went somewhere, because
Cruz beat the throw to first, thereby avoiding the double play and

keeping the inning alive for us. And Nunez had moved to third on the play.

Laker came to the plate next and slapped a single to center, and Nunez came home with the first run of the game. In baseball, the team that scores first wins 65 percent of the time. If the nick of time that got away had not gotten away from the Cubs infielders, Laker would not even have come to the plate, and there would be no score. As it is, the home team is up a run. This is why they practice these simple things, over and over.

THIS DANCE THAT WE DO TOGETHER, MY DAUGHTER and I, or one much like it, is how Derek Jeter, a kid who loves baseball, got to be Derek Jeter, the All-Star shortstop for the New York Yankees. It is how all big leaguers become big leaguers.

Not all big-league shortstops are great ones, but none of them are bad ones. There are good ones, there are great ones, and there are legends. But whichever one they are, they got that way by repeating the steps in the dance, over and over again, day after day, for years and years.

When you watch a professional batting practice, you watch some of the best players in the world, doing the dance over and over. You watch their feet move quickly and surely, you watch their hands react instantly to a small white object that is flying toward them. You watch their arms snap the throws across a diamond or over the outfield grass. You watch them set themselves to be ready for what comes next and you watch them turn and break for the bag at the crack of the bat. You watch them do it over and over again because that is what it takes to get good at it, good enough to stay in the game. You begin to realize that they do this dance so beautifully because they practice it so faithfully.

When I watch these gifted men who play baseball for a living—and when I watch the young women who play on the ball team with my daughter, and the Little Leaguers who play at the school yard behind my son's school, or any ballplayers who are practicing this dance—I think of the steps in my own dance, the dance that is part and parcel of the game to which I have been called, the game that has gripped me, as Jim Bouton might say.

And I am reminded that in order to do those steps well, no matter whether I am playing in the big leagues or the not-so-big leagues, and that is generally where I play, if I want to do these things well enough to play the game with some degree of art and joy and grace, then I must do them over and over and over, every day. I must practice the simple and spare elements of the game that has gripped me if I ever hope to become good at it. And if I do them some more, I might even get better at it. And if I do them some more, I can keep my place in the game itself.

How Did Abraham Do Yesterday?

I was counting on the game's deep patterns, three strikes, three outs, three times three innings, and its deepest impulse, to go out and back, to leave and return home, to set the order of the day and to organize the daylight.

A. BARTLETT GIAMATTI
The Yale Alumni Magazine

CUBS 2ND *(Sounds 1, Cubs 0)—Hatcher walks to open the inning. Zaleta homers to left center, scoring Hatcher from first. Mathews pops up to Cruz at first base. Johns homers to right on the first pitch. Encarnacion strikes out swinging. Norton grounds out to Patterson at third for the third out. (2 runs, 2 hits, 0 errors, 0 LOB)*

SOUNDS 2ND *(Sounds 1, Cubs 3)—Brede singles to open the inning. Patterson walks, moving Brede to second. Baptist bunts to sacrifice, moving Brede to third and Patterson to second. Redman flies to Mathews in left center for the second out (sacrifice), scoring Brede from third; Mathews misses the cutoff man on the play and Patterson takes third base on the throw. Nunez walks, leaving runners at the corners with two outs. Wehner singles to Gonzalez in right field, scoring Patterson; Nunez goes to third. Cruz strikes out swinging for the third out. (2 runs, 2 hits, 0 errors, 2 LOB)*

THERE ARE AT LEAST
three different ways to watch a ballgame.

One is to watch it almost casually, content to sit in the sun or in the cool night air, taking in the sounds and the action and the unfolding of the game itself as a kind of disinterested observer, or at best, an entertained spectator. You sit in the stands and your eye jumps from place to place and you cheer from time to time and you talk to your neighbor from time to time. You pretty much catch only the big moments when they happen. The home run, the stolen base, the fly ball that almost gets over the wall and out of the park, the strikeout on a 3-2 pitch with two outs and two runners on—these things you see happen because you hear the crowd roar or groan and you turn your head to see what you have almost missed.

Another way to watch the game is on foot. This particular way of watching means that you spend about three innings in line at the concession stands, another three innings with your back to the game while you go up the stairs to the concession stands or with your eyes on the stairs as you return. The other three innings of it you spend in your seat asking the next guy what happened and telling him about how you were standing in line when somebody hit a home run, as though you were the only person that it had ever happened to.

The last way to watch a ballgame is the best way, or at least I think it is. It is to get a scorecard and a pencil and keep score as the game progresses. Keeping score is not just a matter of keeping up with who is ahead, it is to keep track of everything that happens on the field, making little shorthand notes on a scorecard.

"Scorers properly feel," notes Ed Munson, the official scorer for the California Angels, "that they are part of the game being played in front of them." It keeps you in the game, it makes you feel as though you are actually part of it. For many of us, the best thing in the world would be to actually be on the field playing the game. For some of us, the next best thing is to participate in it by at least keeping up with it.

Keeping score also gives you a real incentive to stay in your seat and away from the long arm of the vendors selling expensive ballpark stuff. (The folks who watch the game on foot are either really rich or are on their way to being really broke.) You cannot record what you do not see, and the only way to be sure that you see is to stay in your seat and watch the game.

WE SPENT THE BETTER PART OF THE SUMMER THIS year at Greer Stadium keeping track of a player named Abraham Nunez. He is a middle infielder, a shortstop who also plays some second base. In the first place, we kept track of him because those are the positions that the people in our house who play ball usually play. Those are also the two positions on the field that are the most fun to watch, at least for me. They are involved in two of the prettiest defensive plays of the game, when circumstances warrant it—the double play and the throwing out of a runner who is trying to steal second base. The truth be told, though, we have been following Nunez because *he* is so much fun to watch.

In the middle of the summer we had to be away for almost a month. (Had to is not exactly the truth; we were at the beach most of the time.) While we were gone, Nunez got called up to the Pirates to fill in for their second baseman, who was on the injured list. We were checking our e-mail one day at the beach house and checked the Sounds score from the night before, and discovered that he had gone north. So we found ourselves checking the Pirates box scores every day to see if he had played the day before and how he had done. He did not do as well as he hoped over the two or three weeks that he was up. He was in Nashville again by the time we got home. We were disappointed for him, but we were happy that we were still going to get to see him play.

I DID NOT GROW UP KEEPING SCORE—IN FACT, UNTIL a few years ago, I had never done it at all.

But one day when I came through the gate and passed through the tunnel toward the stands, I inexplicably said yes when the man offered me a pencil and a scorecard as I stopped to buy a program. It was the summer that my wife and I were courting, and we were at Wrigley Field, and I think I wanted to impress her with my intimate knowledge of the game. Do not laugh, this is a woman who can quote the current earned-run averages of the Braves' starting pitchers most all season. I was taking no chances.

I was in a place in my life in those days when it was very important to get everything down on paper and not miss anything, good or bad, that was happening to me. I was going through a rebirth of sorts, in virtually every area of my life, and things were coming at me so hard and so fast that I was afraid something would get away if I did not take notes.

For health reasons, I was taking all manner of notes about how much I slept and what time I took my medication and what days I was feeling good and what days I was not. The people who were helping me to try to understand the disease called depression, which I had recently discovered I had been living with for a long time, made it clear that such attention would help. I was trying to learn how to live with it and around it and through it and in spite of it, and so I took their advice to heart for the sake of my mind.

For reasons that had to do with circumstance, I was also living my life in a completely different way than I had been for a long time. I was single again and I was trying to learn how to be a father when I was not living in the same house with my children. One of the ways is to show up on time, on the appointed day, just like you said you would, and the best way for me to do that in those days was to be sure that I wrote everything down. I was also working in a big organization for the first time in a long time, and there were tons of meetings to attend and schedules to keep and places to be and details to track. I am not very good at some of those things sometimes, and keeping little charts and such was the only way that I could keep up at all, even as poorly as it turned out that I did.

I was falling in love again too, with this extraordinary and delightful woman who could make me laugh and a lot of other things that I had not done for a while, and she could also make a pretty good guess as to when the runner was going to try for second on a bloop single to left. I did not want to forget any of it. My father once described such courting time as the "time when you cannot get enough words into the air to express how you feel," and for me that also meant that I could not get enough words on paper.

I was also falling in love with life itself again, and with my vocation as a writer. For some of us who write, keeping notes in journals is a way of not losing any of the memories that make up your story. If a writer's work is, as the novelist Ellen Douglas once said, "to bear witness to what one has seen and heard," then you had better take notes. Your life comes at you so fast most days that you can lose your own story before you even have a chance to tell it and to discover its meaning.

I have a friend who lives in Wichita, an artist and poet and singer and teacher, who once listened to me talk about all of the things that I was doing at the time to discover my life again and how I was living it. She is the sort of person who moves through the world and talks and writes with a kind of natural poetic grace, and she was more than a little amused at all the stuff that I was doing to try to keep up with my life and its workings and ways at the time. "Some of us are just little box makers," she would say with a grin as she gently chided me about all the things that I was trying to keep track of.

About three innings into the game that day at Wrigley, making those little marks in those little boxes, and I was hooked on keeping score. Some of us are just little box makers, I suppose, and some of us are born to try to fill them in with little symbols, and I am both.

KEEPING SCORE IS MUCH EASIER THAN IT LOOKS. And much harder, too.

In the first place, it requires that you learn the language of the game, including its very minute detail, so that you can have a grasp of what happened to each batter that comes to the plate. You also have to learn the shorthand for describing the game (1B for a single, HR for a home run, CS for caught stealing, and so forth) so that you can make the appropriate marks in those little boxes. There is not much room for sentences or even for whole words on a scorecard.

It requires that you pay attention to the game all of the time. Each pitch, each move on the base paths, each fielding play has to be recorded if you are to keep up with the story that is unfolding before you. A trip to the concession stand, poorly timed, can cost you three or four batters, and unless you are at the game with friends who are keeping score or at least paying close attention, then you lose track of the day's work for your favorite player altogether. You can end up with the dreaded WW marked on your card for three or four batters in a row.

The WW is a mark invented by Phil Rizzuto, the famed Yankees player turned broadcaster. He said it stands for "Wasn't Watching." It equals "I was not paying attention, I have no idea what happened or how or why or whether or not it was a close play or an easy play or a dumb play."

Keeping score also requires that you be interested in the game and in its players and in how it is played out. The why and how and who of a game has to matter. Not in some cosmic sense, of course, but in the sense of wanting to be able to remember and to understand why this player had a good day or a bad one, how this thing happened or did not, which plays made the difference and which ones did not matter at all.

"Most spectators watch a great play with an interest which, however intense, is forgotten in the thriller of the next inning. They leave the grounds with a hazy idea of a rather enjoyable afternoon, whose main features are scarce refreshed by reading the press accounts of them some hours later," wrote C. P. Stack. "Keeping score remedies all this. It burns the play into memory."

With the scorecard in your hand, you can keep the game in your mind and in your memory in a way. Which is not necessarily all there is to baseball, or life, for that matter—but for some of us, being able to get a grip on our memories, even a tenuous one, matters a great deal.

OUR FAMILY LIVED AT THE FAR NORTHERN END OF A suburban community that was about thirty miles or so north of Nashville, the city where we went to church and went to shows and concerts and movies and such, and where my father went to work each day. In those days, the days before the interstate highway was built, it could take a good forty-five or fifty minutes for my father to work his way through the traffic and get downtown to the office. He would leave very early most mornings, trying to arrive in the city by seven-fifteen or seven-thirty in order to have a jump on the traffic and some time at his desk before the others began to arrive and before the telephones began to ring and before the meetings and conversations that made up his workday began to flow one into the other into this unending stream of talk and talk and talk and more talk.

He also wanted to get himself in position to be able to get out the door by three-thirty or four o'clock in order to beat the traffic home, and to arrive at our place with as much daylight left as possible. His car would come flying down the driveway, down the hill to where our house sat perched in the middle of four and a half acres of land that sloped pretty steeply from the road, the road that you could not see even from the house, down to the banks of the Cumberland River that ran below us. Generally, within fifteen minutes or so he was back out again in his other work clothes, his old pants and shirt and boots, and one of his endless succession of funny old hats that he used to wear to work in the yard. He could go from publishing executive to field hand in almost no time at all.

The place we grew up had been uncleared woods from top to bottom when we first moved there. In fact, before we moved there we spent what must have been the better part of a year working out there on Saturdays and on Sunday afternoons after church. There were trees to cut down and cut up and then drag off to the burn pile. There were stumps to burn out and a rock wall to build along the edge of the lake so that we would not lose too much riverbank to the water gliding by.

Later there was grass to plant and to mow, and gardens and flowers and shrubs to set out and to tend. And a driveway that had to be maintained with drainage ditches so that the gravel did not all go sliding down the hill with every rain. Then there was all the stuff that my father was always building—a couple of patios, a family room in what used to be a garage, a porch, a couple of tree houses, and on and on.

I asked him once, when I was old enough to wonder, why he would get up so early to get downtown just so he could get home early and work like a dog for three or four hours in the yard. It was inexplicable to his teenage son why that would be something that anyone was interested in doing.

He told me that he spent all day long every day pretty much just talking. "Other people at our company make the records, sing the songs, sell the products, and ship the boxes. All I do is talk. If I can get home before dark and work in the yard for a bit, dig a hole, plant a tree, get a few rows of bricks in on the patio, I can do at least one thing each day that I can point to and say that I did it with my own two hands."

For many of us, at the end of our day, it is hard to see or to say what we have done. Many of us live in a world where our work is hard to measure in any sort of concrete way. My work is very much that way, and at the end of a good day's work there is nothing to hold in my hand except a few sheets of paper, a fair number of which may well have to be thrown out the next day, or at some future point. It can be hard to tell a good day from a bad one.

I used to say to myself that when I grew up and had a house of my own, I was going to have a concrete yard. That way I could avoid having to spend long hours working in the yard the way that my father did. (I knew that they were long hours because I spent a lot of them with him.)

I did live in a place or two with concrete yards, apartment buildings in downtown Chicago and later a condominium in Nashville. But eventually I worked my way around to a house with a yard and a lawn to mow and fences to put up and to paint and a studio to build and trees to trim around and a sidewalk to brick in and on and on and on. And I found myself explaining to my kids that I go out and work in the yard because I want to be able to point to something that I did today, something real. They shake their heads in wonder as they push another wheelbarrow full of dirt across the backyard.

On this particular April day, our guy Nunez does a good day's work. In the first he draws a walk, and he goes to second on a walk given up to Wehner. Nunez helped cause Wehner's walk by getting a good lead off first. (He is a good base-stealer and the opposing pitcher knows it, and Nunez distracted him enough that he could not throw strikes to Wehner.) He takes third on a groundout by Cruz and scores the first run of the game on a single by Laker.

In the second he walks again, and with two out, he is running on the three-two pitch to Wehner. Wehner singles and Nunez moves to third. He is left stranded there on a strikeout by Cruz that ends the inning.

The home team is down by a run when Nunez comes to the plate with two out in the fourth. He singles sharply to center. The pitcher does his "I'm afraid Nunez is going to steal" routine again and walks Wehner again, putting the tying run at second. It is not that Nunez stole second, it is more like he conned the pitcher out of it. He is in scoring position, but he is left stranded again.

After the crowd has stretched in the seventh inning and the song has been sung, Nunez leads off our half of the seventh. He squares around unexpectedly and lays down a perfect bunt, surprising everyone in the infield. He is too fast, and the bunt is too perfect. The pitcher simply picks up the ball and stands there with it. Nunez reaches first without a throw even being made.

The pitcher, worried once again about the tying run moving to second on a stolen base, moves Nunez to second anyway by walking Wehner for the third time of the night. The visitors had changed pitchers, but the result was the same. Our big hitter strikes out again, and so does the next man, but the third guy doubles, and Nunez scores easily to tie the game.

If you have a scorecard and you have been paying attention, you know that Nunez has been to the plate four times tonight, and has been on base all four times. He had two walks, two singles, and two runs scored. No home runs, no runs batted in—just a series of little things done well that made the larger thing come out in favor of the home team.

You can see from your scorecard that he also had six chances to make plays in the field and handled all six of them without error. One was a great diving stop behind the bag at second to rob Gonzalez of a sure single. Another, a rare first-baseman-to-shortstop-to-pitcher double play on a ground ball to first, he handled with a kind of routine brilliance. They are the kinds of plays that all shortstops love to make, and the reason that shortstops are so much fun to watch.

All of us middle infielders in the stands, those of us who wear the "good glove, not-so-good bat" label, are happy that we got to see Nunez work tonight.

MY OLD SCORECARDS AND SCORE BOOKS ARE ON A shelf beside my old journals. Next to them is a box of old calendar pages going back some years now. I designed a way of keeping track of my days on those pages, a system that goes well beyond making and keeping appointments. It is complete with little boxes and marks and abbreviations for weather and naps and stuff. For some reason it is important to me to be able to recall whom I wrote a letter to and whom I called and where I went and what I was reading on a given day.

I have to confess that none of this old business ever comes up in conversation. Seldom does anyone want to know how many letters that I wrote in April of 1998 or which books I was reading in September of 1996. Even I am as uninterested most of the time as everyone else would be all of the time. How many hours that I wrote on a given day years ago matters to others about as much as their knowing how many times Nunez, a minor league infielder for a Triple-A franchise, went to the plate and got on base on a weeknight in early spring in 2000.

I cannot to this day give much of an explanation for my interest in keeping track of such things. If someone was to ask me to defend it, I would not have much to say, except that I must not want to miss anything. Or maybe that I want to be sure that I know what I did today or yesterday, so that I can point to it sometime and say "this is what I did today." Here it is, the real stuff that I spent my day doing.

"There is no shortage of good days," writes Annie Dillard. "It is good lives that are hard to come by." I think that she is probably right. I also think sometimes that the only way to have a good life in any sort of meaningful way is to be able to put a string of good days together more than once. This day and that one and the next one have to be measured against the others in the same way that a ballplayer's statistics mount up over the course of a game and the course of a season and the course of a career. Others can keep all of that in their heads, I guess. But not me.

There is another way to think about it, though. Maybe I keep track of all of these little things in my life because sometimes I wish that I could reduce my days to a box score. Perhaps deep within me there is something that cries out for a way to get to the end of a day and to be able to say how many opportunities I had today at the plate and actually got on base. Or how many times the ball came my way and was handled perfectly, smoothly, gracefully.

Sometimes I wonder if my days should be measured by how many times I answered a hard question from my kids with grace and humor and joy. Or by how many times something difficult came my way and I made the right decision and then followed through. Or by how many times I made the routine plays so that things kept moving along in the corner of the world for which I am responsible. And by how many times the ball came my way and I dropped it.

There are no box scores in the newspapers for how we spend our days, though perhaps it would not be such a bad idea. It would be nice to be able to see that I went 2-for-4 with a sacrifice and that I helped to bring somebody home and that I had a couple of assists. It would be noted that I struck out a couple of times, but everybody does that. And that I only made one error in six chances and it turned out not to cost us anything anyway.

To be honest, I am probably glad that no one is ever going to look up my stats at the end of the season to set my salary or to see if I am to be traded. I think that I cannot be traded at my house—I have the car keys—but one never knows.

I am keeping track of all of these things only for myself. And from time to time, for whatever reason, I find myself looking back to see what took place on an average Thursday in April or Wednesday in September. And I keep going to the ballpark and practicing my little box making. And learning to pay attention to the little things and how they contribute to the larger things.

Just in case someone ever asks, I want to be ready to say what took place. I want to be able to remember whether those were good days or bad. At the very least, I do not want to admit that I was not paying attention at all and that I had to mark them "WW."

IT COULD BE,
IT MIGHT BE . . .
IT IS . . .

. . . now he looks over some low stuff unworthy of him and then, uncoiling, sends one out, straight on a rising line, over the center-field wall, no cheap Fenway shot, but all of it, the physics as elegant as the arc the ball describes.

A. BARTLETT GIAMATTI
The Yale Alumni Magazine

CUBS 3RD *(Sounds 3, Cubs 3)—Myers strikes out. Ojeda grounds out to Wehner at second. Gonzalez grounds out to Nunez at shortstop to end the inning. (0 runs, 0 hits, 0 errors, 0 LOB)*

SOUNDS 3RD *(Sounds 3, Cubs 3)—Laker homers off the left-field foul pole. Brown grounds out to Ojeda at shortstop. Brede fouls out to Hatcher in left field. Patterson grounds out to Zaleta at first (unassisted) for the third out. (1 run, 1 hit, 0 errors, 0 LOB)*

By THE TIME THAT WE
get to the third inning at Greer, there have already been two home
runs. But the faithful were not much interested in either one of
them, even though one of them looked for a moment like it was
going to go over the guitar, which is always something to see.
This was partly because the pair of them, combined with a leadoff walk, have put the home team behind by two runs. We would
get the runs back later, but at the time we did not know that.

The other reason that the two Cubs home runs were not particularly interesting is that we did not get to see the manager yell
at the umpire about either one of them. Which is exactly what we
got when Tim Laker, the catcher for the Sounds, came to the
plate to lead off in the Sounds' half of the third. He is a big, strap-
ping man who plays catcher and first base and who looks more
like a basketball or football player to me. We count on him to hit

the ball hard somewhere two or three times a game. He hit the first pitch right on the nose and it went screaming down the left-field line, rising as it went. It was "like a stream of milk," as broadcaster Bob Costas once called a home-run shot on television.

When it got to the left-field wall it suddenly took a hard left, a ninety-degree left, and bounced down into the picnic areas below the bullpens in left, back behind the stands somewhere. I looked for the ball when I headed toward the parking lot later, but someone had beat me to it.

For some reason, the umpire yelled, "Foul ball." That was when we got to see the manager. Everyone in the ballpark knew that it was a home run. Everyone except the third-base umpire. So, on behalf of all of us, the manager went out, in the spirit of fair play and all of that, to explain it to him.

Being an umpire is not always easy. Ed Runge, who was one of the best, once wrote that "it's the only occupation where a man has to be perfect the first day on the job and then improve over the years." I expect that the Sounds manager was just going out to help the third-base ump improve.

TOWARD THE END OF THE SUMMER OF 1999, NEARLY everyone in the country, baseball fan or not, was talking about home runs. It was the summer of Mark McGwire and Sammy Sosa, the summer of the chase to break the single-season home-run record that Roger Maris of the Yankees had set back in the sixties.

As the summer progressed, both McGwire and Sosa were hitting them at a record pace. McGwire had been hitting home runs in great quantities for years, and most baseball people figured that if anyone had a shot to break the record he was probably the guy. He had been on pace to break the record a time or two in his career already, but injuries had always conspired to cut his season short and he had never made it. For some inexplicable reason, all season long, there was this feeling that this would be the year that the record would fall.

Some other guys chased them for a while, Griffey and Vaughn and a couple more, but by August, it was down to the two of them. People who never really follow the game were checking the sports pages or watching the sports segment of the news to see if either man hit one that day. On the news they would show tape of each at-bat by each man, even when neither of them had hit one out. Their strikeouts ended up being replayed on television more than most guys' home runs are, or at least it seemed that way.

Most evenings, though, you would see one of them coil up and then turn on the ball, and then the ball would explode off the bat, and McGwire or Sosa would drop the bat as it wrapped around him on the follow-through. They tell me that home-run hitters know when they have hit one the instant that they hit the ball. That is how they know to go into their home-run trot.

The home-run trot is the sort of half-jog that all baseball players use when they round the bases after hitting one out of the ballpark. There is a kind of etiquette for it.

The rule is that you keep your head down, careful to act sort of modest and workmanlike about it. A hitter has to be careful about showing up the opposing pitcher. In the first place, the hitter is likely to have to face him again in a couple of innings, and pitchers do not take kindly to having been embarrassed. If you show up a pitcher after a home run, you can almost guarantee that you are going to get a close-up view of a baseball at ninety miles an hour the next time you come to the plate against him. The view will be a little closer than usual because the ball will be thrown in the general direction of your head.

In the second place, one of your teammates, the one who is in the on-deck circle watching you go around the bases, is going to face the pitcher in about thirty seconds. The pitcher is already angry that you hit his pitch out of the park. Your teammate already knows that the odds are pretty good that he is going to get brushed back (that is what they call it, anyway). There is no need to make it worse. If you do, your teammate will take it up with you when you are both back in the dugout.

The last reason for the home-run trot is that you have to be sure that you touch all the bases. If you hit the ball out of the park, it is still not a home run until you touch them all. If you miss one, and the umpire notices it and someone on the opposing team does too, the opponent can throw the ball to the base that you failed to touch, someone can step on the bag, and you are called out. I have seen it happen a couple of times. I suspect that it is more than a little embarrassing to have been good enough to hit the ball three or four hundred feet and dumb enough to have failed to touch all the bases while you were trotting around basking in all the glory.

I do not actually know much about the home-run trot from personal experience. In all the baseball games that I ever played in when I was young, I actually never hit one over the fence. As a home-run hitter, I am 0-for-5—five decades, that is.

WE ARE IN WRIGLEY FIELD IN THE SEPTEMBER OF the great home-run chase. The season is winding down. The two teams that I root for the most, the Yankees and the Braves, are in good shape to secure playoff spots and are beginning to rest their regulars here and there for a day or two so that they will be in good shape for the inevitable, or so it seems, World Series matchup between the two teams.

My son sometimes says that he does not even want to watch the Series these days; it is always between the Yankees and the Braves, and he wants to see someone else have a chance for a change. He is a sweet boy, with a good heart, and I understand what he means. On the other hand, as long as the Series is between my two favorite teams, I am guaranteed to be able to spend the winter basking in the glory of yet another championship. If the Braves and the Yankees make the Series, then I am guaranteed to be a winner. I do not get many guarantees like that.

At this late date, something extraordinary is happening in Chicago. The Cubs, who are generally out of the playoff picture well before the All-Star break, are actually still in the hunt. It has been a long time since they have been close to the playoffs, and there is an added air of excitement to the day as we arrive at the ballpark. But the real excitement has to do with Sammy Sosa.

As we head into the gates and through the turnstiles and up the long inclines toward our seats, Sosa stands at 60 home runs, tied with Babe Ruth on the all-time list, just one back of Roger Maris.

Mr. McGwire has already done the unthinkable a few days before. He tied and then broke the thirty-eight-year-old record for most home runs in a single season. After years of being the most powerful home-run hitter in the majors, and the odds-on favorite to be the one to break the record, he has finally done it. To have two players this close reminds a lot of us that Mickey Mantle chased Roger Maris all through the 1961 season as well. As happy as we were for McGwire, most all baseball fans were cheering for Sammy Sosa to break the record too.

Sammy is a couple of homers behind McGwire now, but they have been going back and forth like that all year. And it is cool today, which means the ball travels faster when it is hit, and the wind is blowing out to left field pretty hard. Today is the sort of day on which Sammy could hit one out even if he is having a bad day, and everybody knows it. Today is the sort of day that one can expect to hear Harry Caray's famous home-run call at least once: "It could be, it might be . . . it is . . . a home run for Sammy Sosa."

The ballpark is jammed when we get there and tickets are hard to come by. Usually, when I am circling the stadium with my hand in the air, looking for tickets, I hold out until we get seats down low in the field boxes, on the first-base side, so that I can see everything better. Today, I am taking no chances. Between the pennant fever and the home-run fever I could walk around looking for good seats until the game is over. I settle for two reasonably good ones, first-base side, second deck. They are not great seats, but it beats not being there. We manage to get in and get settled in time to see him, Sammy that is, come out of the dugout as the announcer roars, "Ladies and gentlemen: Your Chicago Cubs."

The Cubs come up out of their dugout, and the crowd gets to its feet with a roar. Most of the players are in a modified sort of

home-run trot as they head for their positions. They jog gracefully across the field. They skip over the baselines, careful not to
disturb the chalk (superstition runs deep in baseball, no matter at
what level it is being played), and start to re-rake their spots in the
dirt with their spikes, even though the grounds crew has just left
the field. They each have their routines—touching the bag, or
tipping their cap to someone in the stands, or waving to a certain
section of the stadium where someone has a banner up with their
name on it.

Sammy's out-of-the-dugout-and-onto-the-field routine is currently the best in baseball. It is not quite as cool as the great Ozzie
Smith's was—he used to trot to his position at shortstop in Busch
Stadium and turn a back flip for the Cardinal fans—but Mr. Sosa
has a pretty good one. He comes out of the dugout at full speed,
running flat-out toward his position in right field. Then, just
when you think he is going to pull up and turn around to face
home plate, he breaks into his home-run trot and he raises his cap
and jogs along the warning track from right field to center field
and back, waving at the fans in the bleachers, the folks who sit
out there in the sun and the wind and the rain and the cold and
hope for a ball that comes off his bat to land in their glove or their
hands or their lap or their beer. He loves them and they love him.
His joy and their joy at simply being here, in this ballpark, on this
day, is palpable. He taps his chest with his two fingers, the way
that we always see him do after a home run, and then he blows
kisses to them, and they roar back. "Sammy, Sammy, Sammy,"
they chant.

Sammy has become for a lot of us a larger-than-life version of
the sort of heroes that many ballplayers are in fact: good people,
playing a boy's game and grateful for it, who do their work and

play their game with joy and dignity and affection. Some of them play it better than others, and most all of them play it with joy, but few of them have the personality that Sammy does, and so we cheer for the Sammys when they come along, sometimes realizing that in a way we are cheering for all of those who do what they do with gratitude and affection and grace, whether they are ballplayers or teachers or poets or priests or parents or bricklayers.

SOME HOME RUNS ARE LEGENDARY TO A BASEBALL fan. They are the home runs that won a game or a Series, sending one team and its fans to the top of the world and the opposing team and its fans to the depths of despair. Some of them are so famous that even non-baseball fans know them.

In 1951, a light-hitting infielder named Bobby Thomson hit a home run in the ninth to give the Giants a playoff-game win over the powerful Brooklyn Dodgers and catapult the Giants into the World Series. All baseball fans—and most everyone else on the planet, it seems—have seen the grainy black-and-white film of Thomson leaping up and down on his way around third toward home, hats and confetti and programs flying through the air from all over the ballpark, his teammates crowded around home plate in a knot waiting for him to touch them all, with announcer Russ Hodges shouting at the top of his voice, "The Giants win the pennant, the Giants win the pennant," over and over and over.

A woman I know who grew up in New York told me about being at that legendary game. "You got to be there?" I murmured back with more than a little awe in my voice. "What's so good about it?" she said. "The Dodgers lost."

There is another of those black-and-white home runs that a lot of us remember. It is the one that Bill Mazeroski of the Pirates hit over the left-field wall to send my beloved Yankees home without the trophy from the 1960 World Series. I still see the ball hanging over the wall in left field. It was a walk-off home run—a ninth-inning home run to take the lead in the home half of the inning, ending the game, and so everybody just walks off the field. It is the worst kind of home run, if the other team hits it.

Mazeroski was a wonderfully talented second baseman who turned more double plays than anyone in history. Had he not broken my heart, I would have loved him as a player. As it is, I can barely speak his name. How could he have done it? We were in our fourth-grade classroom when it happened. We all groaned when he hit it, and so did my buddies next door in Ms. Anderson's room—I could hear them. I still do not believe that he did it. Mickey Mantle said later that he cried all the way home to Oklahoma after the game. I cried all the way home from school the same day.

In 1988 the Dodgers are playing the Oakland Athletics in the Series. The Athletics are about nine times better than everybody that year. The Series opens in Los Angeles, and the Dodgers, who have no chance, according to everyone who knows the game, are now without their best hitter. Kirk Gibson has hurt his legs so badly that he cannot play. He cannot run at all, and he is out of the lineup for the first game, probably for the whole Series.

In that first game, in the bottom of the ninth, the Dodgers are trailing 4–3 with two outs and one runner on base. The A's have their ace relief pitcher, the best closer of all time, Dennis Eckersley, on the mound to close out the game. For the whole season—

and for a lot of seasons, for that matter—when the A's brought in Eckersley, the opposing team was finished. He was virtually un-hittable. Maybe Gibson could hit him, but Gibson was hurt.

Vin Scully, the velvet-voiced Dodgers broadcaster, is calling the game for television and he begins to get reports from Bob Costas in the Dodger clubhouse that Gibson has left the bench and is back in the clubhouse taking swings and getting ready to hit. Which is impossible, of course; he can hardly walk, much less stand in against Eckersley. As the story is told later, Gibson tells Tommy Lasorda, the Dodger manager (who knows enough about good stories to keep telling this one even if it is not true) that he is going to pinch-hit for whoever is supposed to bat. Lasorda sends word back that Gibson isn't going to do any such thing, and then Gibson appears, and starts taking swings in the on-deck circle. Lasorda has the lineup change given to the umpire, and Gibson limps to the plate while the Dodger fans begin to go berserk.

Eckersley throws five pitches and Gibson never takes the bat off his shoulder; he just watches them. I think I remember Scully saying that Gibson had better hit it out of the park because he sure cannot run to first. With the count 3-and-2, Gibson does exactly that. He stands there for a second, watching the ball disappear into the right-field stands, and then with a grin on his face he slowly starts limping around the bases. He has to touch them all. And right now, the 360 feet that he has to travel looks like a long way. As he rounds first, Scully keeps saying over and over, with no small amount of wonder in his voice, "I can't believe what I just saw. I can't believe what I just saw." None of us can, and neither, for a moment, can Gibson. He heads toward second and it suddenly hits him, or so it seems, and he begins pumping his fists with each stride. Even Eckersley knows that the overstepping of the unspoken boundaries of home-run-trot etiquette is acceptable here. The A's never recover from the shock, and the Dodgers take the championship. It is Gibson's only at-bat in the Series.

Years later Eckersley will say, "It's like the Kennedy assassination. Everyone I see comes up and tells me where they were and what they were doing when Gibson hit that home run." I remember exactly where I was.

For Red Sox fans, the most famous home-run trot of all belongs to Carlton Fisk. It is the only home-run trot I ever saw that started with a dance. The Red Sox, like the Cubs, manage to get themselves in a World Series about as often as Halley's Comet drops by. How two teams with such storied history and such remarkable players, such wonderful ballparks and such glorious fans, cannot finish on top more often is a mystery that will never be solved. To be a Cub fan or a Red Sox fan is to live your life knowing that your day may never come. "Spring," wrote longtime and long-suffering Cub fan George Will, "is the winter of the Cub fan's soul."

But this is not spring, it is October of 1975, in the twelfth inning of game six of the series, the one that Boston must win or the series will be over. The game is tied when Carlton Fisk comes to the plate for Boston, and he is a power hitter, he can hit one out of here and everyone knows it.

He lofts a towering fly ball toward left field. To hit a home run to left in most ballparks you have to get it twelve to fifteen feet up in the air, and hit it at least 325 feet. At Fenway, you only have to hit it 315 feet, the shortest distance in the major leagues. But it has to be something like forty feet up in the air to get over what is known as the Green Monster, the left-field wall. I do not know why the architect designed it that way, but he did. And all right-handed power hitters who have ever played there have been angry at the guy ever since. If you get it up in the air high enough, the wind that comes in off the bay can blow the ball back in, or blow it foul.

As all home-run hitters do, Fisk drops the bat at the sound of the hit. He knows he has hit it hard enough. He also knows that if it goes over the wall, he will get to play tomorrow; if it does not, he will have to clean out his locker. It starts toward foul territory and he begins to lean to his right to bring it back in. Then he begins to jump up and down, and wave the ball out with both hands, looking for all the world like he is telling the pilot of an airliner to straighten up the wheels. Then it starts to drift foul again, so he starts to wave to the right to bring it back into play. Then it seems to occur to Fisk that if the ball does not go over the wall, he is going to need to be on first when it comes down or else he is liable to be thrown out on a 290-foot grounder. So now he is hopping up the line toward first, waving at the ball with both hands, trying to get it to go farther and straighter by sheer force of will. It is one of the classic baseball moments of all time: big, strong, Hall of Fame–bound Fisk, hopping and waving and screaming—and praying, I expect—that the ball will clear the Green Monster. And it does, and the Red Sox live for another day.

AT THE BEGINNING OF THE BASEBALL SEASON, TWO or three days a week my kids and I will go to a ballpark and take batting practice. We have a bucket of softballs for my daughter and a bucket of baseballs for my son, and I will do my best to get the pitches over the plate so that they can work on their swings before the tryouts come. In Little League, you have to go through tryouts and you want to look good so that you get drafted by the coaches who are likely to have the best teams.

My son also pitches, so his sister and I take turns hitting so that he can get some work in off the mound because throwing strikes is both easier and harder when there is a batter in the box. When you have not done it in a day or so, you have trouble concentrating on the plate; when you have not done it in a few months, you have trouble even finding it.

I was not much of a power hitter when I played. The only home runs that I ever hit were of the hard-line-drive-to-right-field variety, the ones that take a funny hop and get past the right fielder, and then get kicked when he tries to pick it up and throw it home. It always helped if his throw took about three hops before it got back to the infield too. I learned to close my hitting stance so that I could try to hit it in that direction every time. In Little League, generally speaking, the weakest infielder was always put at second base and the weakest outfielder was put in right field, and his arm was generally weak too. If you hit the ball to the right side and it cleared the second baseman, you could see it as you ran to first and you knew if the right fielder had fielded it cleanly. If he had not, you could keep running and know you had a shot to make third because of his weak arm. When you rounded third you could see if he was still out there floundering around or if the second baseman had the ball yet, and you could tell if a throw had a chance to beat you to the plate. From time to time, I got a home run on just such a play, sliding across home plate in a cloud of glory and dust.

The second year I played, the Civitan Club put up the money

for a real fence in the outfield, and put me out of the home-run business. I could still hit it through somebody from time to time, but now the fence caught it for him and it was hard for me to get much farther than third.

It is two springs ago, and I am at the plate and my son is pitching. My daughter is standing nearby, and I am demonstrating how you close your stance to hit to the right side to move the runner from second to third. Then I open my stance to show her how that will affect the direction of the ball when it is hit. Sometimes you want to hit it to the left side to give yourself a better chance to beat out anything hit to an infielder. I open my stance, here comes the pitch, and I make contact with what is, at best, a sixty-mile-per-hour fastball. But I get all of it. It turns out that the real hitters are absolutely right: you can tell it is gone when it hits the bat.

Let the highlight reel begin.

WHEN LAKER HITS THE SCREAMER OF A HOME RUN to left, everybody in the Sounds dugout comes up off the bench and everybody in the stands comes up out of their seats. And when the umpire calls the ball foul, the manager, who is coaching third base, heads straight toward the umpire who made the call. He only has to travel about ten or twelve feet to get to him, and he is in the umpire's face before the ball stops rolling around behind the fence that runs along left field behind the bullpen.

Somehow the umpire got turned around as he was turning to look at the ball's flight, and he did not actually see that the reason that the ball ended up behind the left-field bullpen was that it hit the foul pole. Now, when a ball hits the foul pole, it is a fair ball. No one knows why the nomenclature is so odd, but there it is.

The manager pointed this out to the umpire, who just started shaking his head and walking away. Which led to the manager's enumeration of the umpire's multiple sins and possibly the umpire's questionable ancestry as well for a few minutes while stomping his feet. It was the sort of conversation in which the umpire generally digs in and will not change his mind, and the manager ends up watching the rest of the game from the clubhouse after being thrown out of the game for his sins. Fortunately for all concerned, with the possible exception of the Iowa pitcher who was hoping to have his pitching mistake be counterbalanced by an umpiring mistake, the plate umpire came out and told the other umpire what had happened and the call was corrected. The third-base umpire put his hand up in the air and waved his right index finger in a circle two or three times to indicate that it was indeed a round-tripper. And everybody sat back down. Everybody except Laker.

Laker had been finishing up his home-run trot the whole time that the conversation was going on behind third base. He had a very nonchalant air about him, as though he was not really worried about any of it anyway. He has hit quite a few balls over quite a few fences in his lifetime. This particular one came at a good time, but it is only April and it is only the fourth inning, and so it warranted a pretty modest trot. He said later that he knew it was a home run and that regardless of the outcome of the conversation between the manager and the umpires he was going to touch them all anyway. One cannot blame him; if one hits a ball like that, one ought to be able to trot the bases and take one's bows, even if the umpire decides that it is nothing more than a long strike, even if you have to come back to the plate and try it all over again.

THAT DAY IN CHICAGO, MR. SOSA COMES TO THE plate in the Cubs' half of the fifth. Mark Grace has singled to lead off the inning and is on first. The first pitch is a strike. The next pitch is a high fly ball toward left center field. For the briefest of moments there is silence. Then it is clear to all of us, all of us rising to our feet, and all of the ones in the dugout who have scrambled up off the bench to get out to the edge of the dugout to see it fly, that it is going over the wall. It was clear first to Sammy, and you can tell because he has instantly dropped his bat and taken that funny little hop that he takes as he starts off toward first on his home-run trot.

It is no ordinary home run, this one. It is number 61. He, too, has caught Maris now. We in the stands who cheer, we who have seen many home runs in this very park, have seen baseball history being made right in front of us.

Sammy touches them all, head down, running not too fast, not too slow, doing nothing to show up the pitcher while he makes his way around the diamond, trotting as though this was just some accident and that he did not mean to do it. His teammates greet him at the plate and in the dugout, and he flashes that big grin of his. The crowd keeps cheering, and the next batter waits before getting into the batter's box. The umpire waits for a moment, and even the pitcher does, too. After a few seconds, Sammy pops up to the top step and tips his cap to the crowd.

In a little while, not quite an hour, the shadows have covered the field and the stands, except for a couple of spots in the left-field bleachers, when Sosa comes to bat again in the ninth. The Cubs are down two runs. With one out and the bases empty, the count goes to two balls and one strike. The next pitch comes to Sammy and he redirects its flight. Suddenly it is headed toward left field. We stand, all of us, and watch in wonder. It is breathtaking, this one, high and majestic, over the outfield, over the ivy-covered wall, over the bleachers and the Bleacher Bums themselves, and finally over the fence out of sight into the street below the stadium.

"Any minute, any day, some players may break a long-standing record," wrote Connie Mack. "That's one of the fascinations about the game—the unexpected surprises." This one was not totally unexpected by the time September rolled around that year, but it was breathtaking to have been there when it happened.

Sammy has broken the record, hit number 62, and he gives us his little hop and his trot begins, and we stand in our places and cheer and clap and cry at the sheer joy of it.

THERE WAS NO CROWD ON HAND THE DAY THAT I HIT my son's fastball over the fence at the Little League field. There was not even a game. It was just me and my son and my daughter. But I did all of the things that I knew to do; I had never hit one over the fence before, and I was not about to miss the chance to touch all of the bases. It does not count if you do not touch all of the bases.

First, I did the little Sammy Sosa hop as I started out toward first. I could hear Harry Caray in my head: "It could be, it might be . . ." Since I could hear him, I thought that my children should be able to as well. "It could be, it might be . . . it is . . . a home run for Robert Benson," I shouted as it began to drop from the sky.

Closer to first, I started into a little Carlton Fisk, even though the ball was to dead center and there was no wind and there was no chance of its going foul and I was going to count it even if it did. I had actually already seen it as it landed on the track behind the center-field fence and bounced high into the air toward the little grove of trees.

Turning toward second and rounding toward third, I went into my Kirk Gibson, pumping my arms with each step as though I were winning a World Series game. (Actually, Mazeroski had a nice little bit of business going to third that I remembered but could not bring myself to do.) Finally I am rounding third and I am heading for home and I am jumping up and down, yelling, "The Giants win the pennant, the Giants win the pennant, the Giants win the pennant!"

As I cross the plate I notice that my kids are staring at me in some mixture of confusion and bemusement. There is likely some measure of gratitude in their faces as well, gratitude for the fact that none of their friends are here to see this rather extraordinary display of strange behavior by their father. They would not recognize most of the steps in the home-run dance or the home-run trot that I am doing, of course. I know that they may have seen Sammy's hop but they do not know Fisk or Gibson or Mazeroski or Thomson. They have never heard Harry Caray, or Vin Scully either. I have only heard Russ Hodges on tape myself. They have no black-and-white home-run memories that run through their heads, and as far as I know have never been allowed to watch the World Series in a classroom. They have also not yet waited forty-eight years to hit one over the fence.

For one of the few times in my life, I simply do not care what they think. I have hit nothing but ordinary singles most all of my life, enough of them that I know that it is meet and right to celebrate when the extraordinary has come to visit. And for once, I am going to be the guy who tips his hat to the crowd.

"It could be, it might be . . ." It is, it is, and I am ready.

MIGHTY CASEY
ARE US

A man on a hill prepares to throw a rock at a man slightly below him, not far away, who holds a club. First, fear must be overcome; no one finally knows where the pitched ball, or hit ball, will go. Most of the time control, agility, timing, planning avert brutality and force sport. Occasionally, suddenly, usually unaccountably, the primitive act of throwing or striking results in terrible injury. The fear is never absent, the fear that randomness will take over. If hitting a major league fastball is the most difficult act in organized sport, the difficulty derives in part from the need to overcome fear in a split second.

A. BARTLETT GIAMATTI
Baseball and the American Character

CUBS 4TH *(Sounds 4, Cubs 3)—Hatcher strikes out swinging.*
Zaleta singles to Brede in left. Mathews homers to score Zaleta and
the Cubs regain the lead. Johns doubles down the left-field line to
Brede. Encarnacion grounds out to Patterson at third. Norton
strikes out for the third out. (2 runs, 2 hits, 0 errors, 1 LOB)

SOUNDS 4TH *(Sounds 4, Cubs 5)—Baptist is called out on*
strikes. Redman flies out to Mathews in center field. Nunez singles
to Mathews in center. Wehner walks, Nunez goes to second. Cruz
strikes out to end the inning. (0 runs, 1 hit, 0 errors, 2 LOB)

I WATCHED A GIRL ONCE who had just joined a YMCA recreational-league team. It was her first practice and maybe even the first time that she had played any organized baseball at all. She was a little nervous about the whole deal, or at least it seemed that way to me. And who can blame her?

She was nine or ten years old, she had some shoes with cleats on them and a glove and a hat, but after that she did not seem to have much of the stuff that it takes to be a ballplayer, and she had no experience to boot. She seemed shy and a little lost, as though her days of playing catch with her father in the backyard and watching other people play the game had not really prepared her for being on the field. She was not a very big girl either, and she looked to be getting smaller by the minute. And to be sure, the boys on the team, the ones who had played before, were all looking at her a little funny when she showed up for practice. There was one other girl on the team and she had been playing for a couple of years, but the novelty of having a girl on your baseball team had still not worn off for most of them.

It seemed to take the coach by surprise too; he must have been faked out by her name or something and did not realize that he had drafted another girl to put on the team. When the team got ready to practice taking infield, he sent the new girl out to work at second base with the older girl. Older girl, I say; she was ten, maybe eleven at the most.

I watched them for a minute or two. The older girl was talking to the younger girl with a kind of veteran-to-rookie countenance and the whole time she was talking she was smoothing out the dirt with the toes of her cleats, the way that ballplayers do. Pretty soon, I saw the younger girl beginning to do the same thing. They kept talking and smoothing out the dirt and the big girl kept telling her stuff. The big girl would point to a base or to the plate as though she was explaining the position or the drill. Then the older girl spit twice, once into her glove and once onto the ground. Then I saw the younger girl do the same.

In a little while, after the practice was over, I made my way over to the older girl, whom I knew, and asked what she was doing out there before practice with the sort of unladylike move that I suspect would have made her mother cringe. "I was teaching her how to spit," she said. "You have to learn or you can't be a ballplayer."

WITH TWO OUT IN THE SOUNDS' HALF OF THE FOURTH, Nunez singles to center and then moves up to second when Wehner draws a walk. Cruz comes to the plate for the Sounds with a chance to drive in a run with a base hit and keep the inning alive.

This game is my first chance to see Cruz play this year. He came into the game as the Pacific Coast League's hottest hitter. The season is young, of course, but to lead the league in home runs, runs batted in, extra, base hits, doubles, and slugging percentage is no mean feat, whether the season is two weeks old or two months old.

Cruz is a big man, powerfully built, with broad shoulders and big hands. He is older than most of the players on the team and moves around the field and the dugout with a more detached air than most of the young guys. There is this sense that you are watching a wily veteran somehow set down here among these boys. There are always some players like that on a Triple-A club.

He has been a journeyman player most of his career, up with a major league team from time to time, and then back down to the minors or traded to another club that needs a left-handed bat to bring in off the bench. He was originally drafted by the Tigers, bounced around in their farm system for a while, and then was traded to the Yankees. He appeared in twenty games for the Yankees, and then he hurt an ankle, went back down to Columbus (their Triple-A franchise) and never made it back up to New York. After they let him go, he hooked on with another team and then another and finally ended up signing with Pittsburgh as a minor league free agent. In Nashville last year, he finished the season second on the club in batting average, home runs, and runs batted in. Which means, of course, that we count on him to get hits with runners on.

In the first inning, he came to the plate with runners at first and second and hit a ground ball that should have been a double play, but he managed to beat the throw to first. He did not bat the run in, but at least he kept the inning alive. In the second he came to the plate with runners at first and second and two outs and proceeded to strike out to end the inning. Now it is the fourth inning with runners at first and second, and so far our cleanup hitter has not cleaned up much at all. We are down two runs and the hottest hitter in the league is due for a hit.

He strikes out again, and the crowd groans. The last swing was wild and late because he was fooled on the pitch. "That was ugly," says the guy in the seat in front of me.

IF YOU ARE GOING TO LEARN TO BE A BALLPLAYER, there are several things that you have to learn about how to look like a ballplayer. One of them, of course, according to my Little League friend, is how to spit.

But there are a lot of other things as well. You have to learn how to carry your batting gloves in your back pocket so that the fingers flop out just right when you are in the field. Too far and they are liable to fall out when you are making a play, too little and it just looks like you are still carrying your wallet.

You have to learn to smooth the dirt around your infield position with your toes, if you are an infielder, and you have to learn to lose your hat off your head in a really cool way when you are chasing a fly ball, if you are an outfielder. I was an infielder and so I do not know how to do that; I never had to learn. But I do know that some guys look cooler losing their hats than others do. The best was Willie Mays, of course.

Then there is the whole crowd of stuff that has to be learned in order to look like a hitter when you go to the plate. You have to learn how to step out of the batter's box and tap your cleats with your bat. You do this to knock the dirt out of them so that you do not slip while you are in the batter's box. I do not think that it actually makes much of a difference unless the field is really muddy, but I do know that it does make you look like a ballplayer.

These days, evidently you have to learn how to hold your hand up to let the umpire know that you are not ready for the pitcher to throw the pitch yet, the way the ballplayers do on television now. Pitchers evidently are less trustworthy now than they used to be, and you have to watch them or they will try to throw it past you while you are still getting back into the batter's box after tapping your cleats. The world is a less civil place than it used to be, I suppose.

You also have to learn to read the signs from the third-base coach, the long and complicated hand signals that they go through to let you know whether they want you to swing away or take a pitch or bunt. The signs let you know as well if the runners on base are going to be stealing or not.

The most important thing that you have to learn about being a batter is the hardest thing to learn of all.

"When you play this game twenty years, go to bat ten thousand times, and get three thousand hits, do you know what that means?" This from Pete Rose, the legendary Cincinnati Red, who finished his career with more than four thousand hits, and more than anyone else in the history of major league baseball. "You've gone zero for seven thousand," Pete said in answer to his own question. Another way to say it is that, at five hundred at-bats a year, you played fourteen years without getting a hit.

That is the hardest thing of all to learn about being a batter:

that most of the time you are going to make an out. And some of the time it is going to be at the worst time possible. And sometimes it is going to be a really ugly strikeout.

"BASEBALL," SAYS MANAGER TONY LARUSSA, "IS THE all-time humbler."

Generally speaking, the team that wins its division in the major leagues will win somewhere in the neighborhood of 85 to 95 games in the course of the season. The other side of that statistic, of course, is that these winners will have managed to lose between 67 and 77 baseball games. You may be winning every other day, but you are pretty close to losing every other day too. "It is not a game that you can play with your teeth clenched," observed George Will.

It is simply a game where defeat and failure go hand in hand with triumph and success. "Those two impostors," as Kipling referred to them once, are never far away from each other or from the ones who play the game.

At a given point this year in the major league season, after 150 or so games had been played, one could check the statistics for the top home-run hitters in the majors and discover that two of the top five were also in the top five in strikeouts. Two of them were leading the league in grounding into double plays, which is something even worse than a strikeout if you ask me. A play that loses two outs is clearly more costly than a play that gives up one out. "Every pitch is a potential home run," said the pitcher Preacher Roe. That is true, but every pitch has more potential to be a strikeout or a double-play ball or a pop fly to left.

"Baseball is the only field of endeavor where a man can succeed three times out of ten and be considered a good performer," said Ted Williams once. He was the last man in the major leagues to hit .400, in fact, and the only one in the modern era of baseball. Hitting a baseball to a place where someone isn't is simply not something that is easy to do.

OUR MAN CRUZ WILL RETURN TO THE PLATE IN THE seventh inning with runners again at first and second and the Sounds down by two runs. It marks the fourth time in the game that he has arrived in the batter's box with runners in scoring position, runners who had done their job to get on base and move up so that the big guy for our team could bring them home. In three tries this evening, he has hit a weak ground ball to second that turned into a force-out by Wehner, and has struck out twice.

When he arrives in the seventh, he is pressing a little. The swings are big and strong, and he grunts with each swing of the bat as though he is trying to kill the ball. "When you are in a slump, it's almost as if you look out at the field and it's one big glove," observed Vance Law, the former Pirate great. Cruz is swinging as though he thinks it will just be easier to hit it over everyone. Which it is not, of course, but whatever he has been trying all evening is not working either. Three giant swings later, he is out. He never even got a piece of it. The best hitter in the league has managed to look like the worst hitter in the league on this particular night. There will be other nights for him when things go better, but for tonight he just has to say, "That's baseball," and head for the house. Maybe not an all-time humbling, but a humbling nonetheless. But he was not the only one humbled on this April night.

The fourth inning alone was enough to have some of the guys muttering to themselves. Four of the outs recorded were strike-outs. Four of the six professional ballplayers who made outs did not even get the bat on the ball. The pitcher wound up, the pitch came in toward the plate, these young men who had spent most of their lives hitting baseballs almost every day of the year, at bat against a couple of pitchers that were, at least on this night, hardly unhittable, and they could not even put the ball in play.

It turns out, at least according to my stats, that in the course of the game, more than two-thirds of the hitters who came to the plate made an out, and nearly a third of the outs were strikeouts. Eighty percent of the outs came on plays in which the hitter hit the ball somewhere between not at all and less than a hundred feet, hardly the sort of thing that the hitter was hoping would happen when he arrived in the batter's box, tapped his cleats, and held up his hand while he was getting settled. They were not ex-actly the sort of herculean blows that one might expect when one goes to see people who get paid to hit a baseball.

And yet there it is. That's baseball.

THERE IS A CUSTOM IN BASEBALL THAT GOES LIKE this: If you are the hitter who makes the third out, or if you hap-pen to be on base when the third out is made, you do not have to go back to the dugout to put your helmet away and get your glove. You just stay put and someone, the closest base coach or the batboy, will come and get your stuff, and then one of your teammates will bring you your glove and your hat from where you left them in the dugout. It is probably to speed up the game, but it seems to me to be the least that they can do. It is already embarrassing enough to have made the third out; they may as well be kind to you.

The worst, of course, is to be left standing there at the plate, after having struck out to end the inning with a runner or two on and your team needing a run or two to retake the lead. You are just sort of standing there by yourself, the other team's catcher having headed for his dugout, and the umpire walking away quickly the way that umpires do, as though they would just as soon not be seen with a guy who just struck out with runners on. The batboy comes out to get the bat and stuff from you, and then you are just sort of there for a minute trying to look as though you know what you are doing.

There are times when a player will stand there jawing with the umpire over whether or not the called third strike was actually a strike. But that does not happen very often or go on for very long. You can be thrown out of the game for arguing balls and strikes with an umpire more quickly than for any other argument.

Other times batters will do the sort of stuff that all of us little boys have done at one time or another when things do not go our way. They will slam the batting helmet down in frustration or sling the bat toward the dugout. They will rip their batting gloves off their hands in a huff, as though certain that the batting gods have somehow singled them out for cruel and unusual punishment. They will act as though they cannot believe that they have managed to strike out and believe that they could not possibly do it again and that it was somehow a cruel trick of some sort that they did it this time.

It always strikes me funny when they act that way. It is not as though they have never made an out before. And if they keep playing the game, they are going to make some more outs too.

WHEN CRUZ GOES DOWN ON STRIKES TO END THE inning, he stands for just a second or two, looking at his bat as though it were the culprit. Then he very calmly bends over at the waist and places the bat gently on the ground. Without straightening up, he takes his batting helmet off and sets it softly beside the bat. He then unfastens the shin guard that he wears on his right leg and lays it in the helmet. Then he pulls his batting gloves off, puts them neatly one on top of the other, and lays them in the helmet as well. As he straightens up, he picks up the helmet and the bat and calmly hands them to the batboy and turns and walks to his position at first base. No runs, no hits, no errors, but then no muttering, no tirades, no whining either.

There are those who would say that they are not quite sure what to think about a ballplayer who has a cool post-strikeout move that he does when he strikes out to end the inning. After all, it would would lead one to suppose that he has struck out quite a bit, perhaps a bit too often even. They are thinking perhaps that he ought to be angry, be remorseful, be something, be anything but placid and calm in the face of defeat.

I am thinking that this is a man who has played the game for many years and knows some of what baseball will teach you if you are willing to listen. I am also thinking that I want my kids to learn to do what he does when they strike out. I am also thinking that maybe I should learn some sort of post-strikeout move myself.

IT WILL NOT BE TOO LONG BEFORE I AM FIFTY YEARS old. I am somewhere in the neighborhood of the seventh-inning stretch, one might say, and I have some of the same sort of mixed feelings about it that all of us do. I am in good health, and even though I am less inclined than a lot of people that I know to spend a great deal of time and energy at a gym somewhere trying to get in shape, there is a better-than-average chance that I am going to go the full nine innings here. No one is making any predictions about my imminent demise, though I know, like everyone else—even those that do not want to admit it—that the game cannot last forever.

The work that has been given me to do—remembering, collecting, and trying to discover the meanings in my story so that from time to time a reader can hold them up to the light and see their own stories a little more clearly—has meant and still means that I spend a fair amount of my time looking backward, looking for bits and pieces of things that tell me something about what it means to be in this game at all. And it means that I remember the days that were not so good as well as the ones that were very good.

One could write a long litany of such days if one were so inclined. There are stories of days that I can remember when my turn at the plate came and I simply struck out. Days when some circumstance presented itself and there I was, expecting to and expected to hit the ball out of the park, and I simply did not come through. Some of the time it had to do with work and other times it had to do with relationships. Sometimes it was family and sometimes it was friends who were counting on me, sometimes it was people far away who for one reason or another were counting on me to come through and I simply failed to do so.

Most of the time, I even knew what to do and just did not get it done. I had read the signs and I had tapped my cleats and I had my helmet on tight and my eye on the ball and I simply swung and missed. There are people that I can name, people who were kind and gracious to me both before and after, who were let down by my failure and whose lives were changed by the fact that I did not come through for them when it mattered. Their chance to come home in some way was taken away by my inability to put the ball in play or keep the rally alive or whatever metaphor you want to stretch and wrestle into shape here. I can see their faces in my memory, and I even still see some of them from time to time, and I still feel bad about not having been able to do what they had counted on me to do.

"You win some, you lose some, and some days you get rained out," goes the old baseball saying. The worst days are when you lose some and it is your own fault. But that's baseball. We are all Mighty Casey and we are all bound to swing and miss sometimes. And sometimes there will be little or nothing that we can do to make up for it all.

It will happen again too, I expect. Sometime here in the late innings, I am going to come to the plate again a few times with a chance to do something good for the home team and I am going to hit a weak ground ball or swing and miss. To think that I am not, that there is not as much chance to fail as there is to succeed, is to pretend that I am somehow different than all the rest of the people in the game. It is to believe that I alone will be able to do what no one else has ever been able to do, and that is to get a hit every time I go to the plate.

MR. CRUZ HAD A TOUGH FEW WEEKS IN NASHVILLE. His numbers did not improve much and then suddenly he was gone. We went away on vacation and we were gone for some time, and when we came back there was a new kid playing first base.

It turned out that Cruz had been called up by the Pirates and spent a few weeks there trying to find a hitting groove that would keep him in the big leagues. But it did not work out there either, and they released him. The last I heard, he was playing for a team in Mexico, far from the big leagues where he had hoped to be able to come through when it counted. He is in the late innings of his playing career now, and he may not be able to get another chance to come back around again. I hope that he does.

There is this other thing that I hope. I hope that from here to the end of the game, whenever it turns out that I am somehow unable to hit the ball cleanly, whenever I am unable to even put the thing in play so that someone will have a chance to come home, whenever I swing and miss, or worse, do not even get the bat off my shoulder and take a swing at the blame thing, that I will have the presence of mind and the grace to simply put my things on the ground and go back out to my position. That's baseball.

DO NOT TURN
YOUR HEAD

Baseball, the opportunist's game, puts a tremendous premium on the individual, who must be ready to react instantly on offense and defense and who must be able to hit, run, throw, field. Specialization obviously exists, but, in general, baseball players are meant to be skilled generalists. . . . Players are also sufficiently physically separated on the field so that the individual cannot hide from clear responsibility in a crowd, as in football or Congress. The object, the ball, and what the individual must do are obvious to all, and each player's skill, initiative, zest, and poise are highlighted.

A. BARTLETT GIAMATTI
Baseball and the American Character

CUBS 5TH *(Sounds 4, Cubs 5)—Myers reaches on an infield hit to Nunez at shortstop. With Ojeda at the plate, Myers is picked off and caught in a rundown and is tagged out by Nunez. Ojeda strikes out. Gonzalez grounds out to Nunez at shortstop to retire the side. (0 runs, 1 hit, 0 errors, 0 LOB)*

SOUNDS 5TH *(Sounds 4, Cubs 5)—Laker grounds out to Johns at third. Brown flies out to Gonzalez in right. Brede grounds out to Johns at third to end the inning. (0 runs, 0 hits, 0 errors, 0 LOB)*

IN THE TOP OF THE FIFTH
at Greer, Iowa's second baseman, Myers, comes to the plate to do what all leadoff hitters are supposed to do: get on base. It is something that he has not accomplished in two tries so far this evening, and one suspects that he is feeling the pressure a bit. His team has a one-run lead, but that is not much; they could use a little insurance. One can almost hear the manager saying to him as he leaves the dugout, "Come on, now, we need base runners." Myers has probably already said it to himself.

Myers pulls a pitch hard on about three hops into the hole between Nunez at shortstop and a diving Patterson at third. At first it looks to be a solid base hit to left. Nunez, however, darts to his right, goes down on one knee, and backhands the ball along the edge of the outfield grass. He comes up throwing, and nearly throws out Myers, who is flying toward first. But Myers is on, in the way that a lot of middle infielders get on base. I know, I had to get on base that way a lot myself.

I was secretly glad to see him get on base. For us "no stick" guys, beating out a ground ball is one of the few things that we can do at the plate that a home-run hitter cannot do.

WHEN I WAS GROWING UP, I FULLY EXPECTED TO BE the second incarnation of Bobby Richardson, the Yankee second baseman. I still think about it from time to time.

"It's the great daydream, an idea that you can never quite give up," wrote George Plimpton. "Always, somewhere in the back of your mind, you believe that Casey Stengel will give you a call." By 1961, the year that I started Little League, Stengel was actually already gone from the Yankees, replaced by Ralph Houk, but I still wonder if I will get a call someday.

Richardson played on maybe the greatest team of all time, certainly one of the greatest New York Yankee teams of all time. It was the 1961 Yankees, the one with the household names. The everyday lineup read RICHARDSON, KUBEK, MARIS, MANTLE, BERRA, HOWARD, SKOWRON, BOYER. With Ford or Terry or Stafford or Sheldon on the mound and Arroyo in the bullpen, and all the rest. They won 101 games that year, and Whitey Ford won an incredible 25 of them. Maris hit 61 homers to break Babe Ruth's record that season, and they took out the Reds in five games in the Series.

Richardson was a great second baseman who, along with Tony Kubek at short, led the American League in double plays. He was a decent hitter, though not really a powerful one. Most years he would hit about three home runs or so and maybe only drive in 35 or 40 runs. But he was coming off an MVP performance in the 1960 Series that he earned with his bat, setting records for most RBIs in the series and in one game.

Those were the days of black-and-white television, at least at my house, and the Yankees were on the Game of the Week virtually every weekend in those days. If you turned on the game and neither team was wearing pinstripes, then you went outside to play ball. But if they were on the screen, then you watched every minute.

I learned as time went by that you were either a Yankee fan or you were not. If you were, then there was no other team. And, of course, there was no other stadium but Yankee Stadium.

"WHEN I WAS A SMALL BOY IN KANSAS, A FRIEND OF mine and I went fishing. I told him that I wanted to be a real major league baseball player, a genuine professional like Honus Wagner. My friend said that he'd like to be President of the United States. Neither of us got our wish." That's right—Dwight Eisenhower never got his call from the big leagues, either.

Once it began to dawn on me that it was not very likely that I was ever going to play for the Yankees, I began to try to find something to do to make myself useful.

My family owned a music publishing business, and I worked in it for a long time. Then my father decided to leave it to write full-time, and it looked as though the business was going to change a lot, and I did not want to go through all of that. I had been there almost ten years, and in many ways, it was time for me to leave it whether my father had stayed or not. It had become harder and harder to pass myself off as a business executive. Yankee pinstripes were not in my future, but a pinstriped suit did not seem to fit either.

I had a friend who lived in Chicago, and he owned a small advertising and marketing firm, and I flew up there and convinced him somehow that I could write such things, and came home and packed to move. For the record, the day after I unloaded the rental truck and moved my stuff into my apartment, I went to Wrigley Field to see the Cubs play. It was my first time there. The next day was my second, and the day after that was my third. My years in Chicago were good to me. I learned how to get paid to write, and I fell in love with ballparks all over again as well.

I spent a couple of years at the agency in Chicago and then went out on my own to do the work on a free-lance basis. I moved back home to Nashville, only to discover that most of my work was in Chicago, and so I flew back and forth all of the time, and eventually the travel got me down. So I went to work at a small agency in Nashville, lasted just a few months, and started my own shop. It only took me about three years to run that into the ground, along with a little book-publishing company that I had started up on the side, and I took a job with a major publishing house again. After two years they let me go, and rightly so. All those years on my own had made me something less than a suitable employee.

And now, whether it is useful or not—something that always remains to be seen—I write books. It is easier than trying to hit a curveball, at least for me, though not as pretty as turning a double play the way that Bobby Richardson could. The fact that I do not have to put on a suit and tie and go to the office is pretty good, but not as good as it would be if my "office" were at second base in Yankee Stadium.

But I did finally get to visit the place.

MYERS IS AT FIRST BASE WITH NOBODY OUT AND IS looking to steal second. It is exactly the sort of thing that leadoff hitters are supposed to do.

He works his lead out a step or two with each pitch that the Sounds pitcher throws to the plate. Baptist is a left-hander, and when he pitches from the stretch, he has a clear view of what Myers is up to the whole time. He throws over to first a time or two to chase him back. Myers keeps stretching his lead between pitches and the throws to first base. The general rule of thumb for a base stealer is that if you do not have to dive back into first base when the pitcher throws over, then you do not have enough of a lead to steal. So Myers keeps inching his way closer and closer to second, keeping his eye on the shortstop, who will be covering if he takes off for second, and checking his feet to see how far he is from the first-base bag.

Somewhere in there, as his head turns just a little from second to the pitcher to first to second again, he misses the fact that Baptist has slipped his back foot off the pitcher's rubber, which means that he can throw to first. When Myers looks up, he sees the ball headed to first, and knows in an instant that he has been picked off. "Don't turn your head, pal," I say under my breath.

MY FIRST TRIP TO THE HOME OF THE NEW YORK YAN-kees came about because my wife does do something useful for a living, and she had to go to New York to do some of that work, and my task was to go along and carry her bags and share her room and eat good food and do my best to be an agreeable traveling companion. It is really fine work if you can get it, though I have to tell you that I will fight you tooth and nail to keep my position. Her job was to go careening around Manhattan for a couple of days calling on the people with whom she was doing business in those days. My most important job after we arrived in New York was to stay in the room and wait for the telephone call that she said we should expect.

Per the instructions, I was to wait to hear from a young woman at a public-relations firm that my wife had worked with who had said that she would try to get us tickets for a Yankees game. So I waited by the phone, just as I was supposed to do. After I had waited through the million hours or so that were between one o'clock and three o'clock that afternoon, the call finally came and I was on my way to Yankee Stadium at last. Game time rolled around and we headed for the subway station, and to tell you the truth, I think my wife was as excited as I was.

We had spent much of our first summer together courting at the minor league park in Nashville. The first gift that she ever gave me was a fitted wool regulation Yankees cap. I am married to a woman who reads books, devours the *New York Times,* is kind and generous to my two children, cooks the best risotto in the city, is somehow convinced that being a writer is a reasonable and honorable thing for me to do for a living, and owns her own book for keeping score at the ballpark. How good is that?

We were both giggling like kids as we rode in the elevator down to the lobby. When we hit the subway station, we could see others headed in the same direction. I was glad to see them. Even though I had spent almost the entire day studying the subway maps, I was deathly afraid that I was going to miss a stop and miss some of the game.

When you go to Yankee Stadium on the subway at night, and the train comes up out of the ground, the stadium appears suddenly: the House that Ruth Built, bathed in light and sort of hovering against the dark sky like something from *Close Encounters of the Third Kind*. My wife just rose up out of her seat at the sight of it, and she was not alone. Then the crowd was surging forward, a temporary community on a pilgrimage together, laughing and grinning, more at ease with one another than big-city folks generally are.

Our instructions for picking up our tickets were to go to the players' entrance. Not the Will Call window, mind you, the players' entrance. My wife knows pretty good folks, I realized, not for the first time. So we went around the stadium to find the right gate. Once through the gate and at the entrance, we found ourselves face-to-face with a very large man with mirrored sunglasses and weight-lifter arms, and a not-so-friendly face. "This is the players' entrance," he thundered down in my direction, it being obvious to him that I had no business at the players' entrance for the New York Yankees. (I think he thundered; I distinctly remember thunder.)

"My name is Robert Benson and my name is on the guest list." The proper word for the way I said that is "meekly."

With a not-quite-convinced scowl on his face he scanned the sheet on the clipboard that he was holding. I, of course, just knew there had been some mistake, and that I was about to be laughed out onto the sidewalk, if not thrown out onto the sidewalk, and all I could think about was whether or not we had enough cash to buy two tickets from a scalper.

"Ah, Mr. Benson. Come in, come in, we were expecting you two. We'll have you fixed right up."

We were ushered through the door and introduced to the assistant general manager as we started down a hall. I do not know who they thought we were, but we were trying to be as nonchalant about it all as we could, trying to act as if we walked through the Yankees' clubhouse all the time. They handed us tickets, and then they gave us two pairs of socks. It was Sock Night at Yankee Stadium, and the first four thousand kids, or some dumb thing like that, and evidently anybody on the clubhouse guest list got a free pair of socks with a Yankee logo on them. Then they gave us programs and scorecards and passed us off to an usher at the end of a tunnel that led up into the field boxes. He chatted us up all the way, as though we must be somebody. Maybe he thinks that one of us is famous, I thought as we walked along.

I DO NOT KNOW MUCH ABOUT WHAT IT MEANS TO BE the star or to be famous or to be well known. Like most people, I only know what I read about it or see on television.

On my Little League team I was known as a kid who had a good glove but no bat, and, to be honest, not much of an arm either. Which meant that I went to the plate hoping for a walk most of the time or hoping that I could beat out the bunt that I was about to lay down. I was fast, and I knew that if I could get on base, then I could steal, but I never was much of a hitter. I could not hit a curveball to save my life, and by the time I got to Babe Ruth ball, I could not hit a fastball either.

I did manage to hustle my way onto the school basketball teams, and played through junior high and high school and even lucked my way into a scholarship at a small college. I was the captain a couple of times and a point guard, the guy who makes sure that the other guys get the ball when they are supposed to and where they are supposed to so that they can score their points and get their names in the papers and be the stars. I am not complaining. With no more size and no more talent than I had, I was just glad to be on the team, and more than happy to get to play every night.

"Anybody with ability can play," observed Bob Uecker about the major leagues. He made this observation after his .200 lifetime hitting career was over. "To last as long as I did with the skills I had, with the numbers I produced, was a triumph of the human spirit." Uecker could have been speaking of my basketball career as well.

I went to a retirement dinner for our old high school coach not too long ago. There were guys there from about twenty years' worth of teams, and our old coach was acknowledging them all. When he got to me, he said, "Now, Benson may not have been as good as some folks, but he came to play every day." Not exactly Hall of Fame stuff, but there it is.

My father was pretty well known in the publishing and music circles that we traveled in, even famous in a way, I suppose. He was the executive vice president of what was then the second-largest religious music publishing house in the world. He was also an ordained minister, and later an author with a pretty fair-sized audience, and he traveled and spoke at retreats and conferences and the like for twenty years or so. Some years he would work as many as twenty-five or thirty weekends a year. There were some places that he went every year to speak where there were huge crowds, and I would have to help sneak him out the back door of the hall so that he could get away and rest before it was time for him to speak again.

In those circles, I was Bob's boy. Not unhappily, not at all. He is still the finest man that I have ever known, the one grown man on the planet that I would rather be with than anyone else. The fact that he has been gone from us for some fifteen years or so now has not changed that at all. But the work that I did with him and beside him and on behalf of the company was behind-the-scenes stuff.

Later, when I did finally stop trying to do other things for a living and settled down to write books full-time, it took about two weeks after my first book came out for my ego to remember what the rest of my brain already knew: that there are fifty thousand books published every year in this country, and that it was not very likely that one of mine was ever going to be the kind of book that somehow got my name in lights anywhere anytime soon. Never, would be a safe guess.

But I did finally find a way to write, and a way of telling my own stories in the hope that whenever I tell them with some measure of honesty and clarity, my readers will come to understand their own stories better. So now at least I get to play the game every day. At my level, it is a little like being a utility infielder, but I do get to wear baseball hats all day whenever I want. I can also throw ball in the afternoon with my kids, and I can make batting practice if I have been to the grocery already, and I can stay up all night and follow the scores on the Internet during the pennant races if I want.

WE COME OUT AT THE BACK OF THE STANDS IN YANkee Stadium and the usher starts leading us down the steps to our seats. We keep getting closer and closer to the field, and we keep grinning at each other as if to say, How good is this? In the end, we are seated on the aisle, right behind home plate, seventeen rows back. The most famous ballpark in the game is now at our feet.

They are finishing the introductions of the starting lineups, and then playing the national anthem, and then the umpire and thirty or so thousand other folks yell, "Play ball," and we settle into our seats again. That is when things started to go badly, or so it seemed to me.

Here I am, in the best place on earth, watching the best team on earth play the best game on earth, and my best friend on earth is suddenly not having a good time. Or at least it seems that way to me. I am pointing things out in the stadium and pointing out ballplayers that we have admired on television and she is hardly even looking at them or listening to me. I try to tell her about stuff that I am finding in the program and she will not even open hers up or look at the pages when I hold them open. I call for the beer man, she passes. I call for the hot dog man, she does not even look at me.

"Are you okay?" I finally ask, in the tiny voice that we all use when we are afraid that we have somehow managed to mess up again.

"Yes," she says in the distracted sort of tone that suggests she is not, and that things will only get worse if I try to do anything about it. I pull my Yankees hat down tighter on my head and stare at the game. An inning and a half goes by with hardly a word between us.

I DID MANAGE TO BE A SEMI-FAMOUS LOCAL ATH-lete for all of one day in high school. My fame spread far and wide, or at least the 20 miles south to Nashville, and another 12 miles north to another of the suburban communities north of the city.

During my junior year, our basketball team played a district tournament game against a school from a few miles up the road. It was in the semifinals and our school was hosting the tournament. We had no right to be in the semifinals; we were not that good. There were two teams in our district that had been ranked in the top five in the state all year long. Somehow we had managed to win a couple of games on our home court and had earned the right to play one of those big teams for the chance to meet the other one in the championship game.

They were big and tall and fast and talented. We were small and quick and lucky. At the end of the game, we somehow managed to put ourselves in a position where if a certain skinny point guard could hit two free throws with about 19 seconds left on the clock, we would win. He did, and the next morning I found myself in a photograph in the sports section of the Nashville paper. I was standing at the free-throw line just about to take the second shot. The headline even had my name in it, though the story was about how the best team had been surprised by the little guys.

For a few minutes it seemed, at least in certain circles, that I was the center of the basketball universe. Unless, of course, you did not go to my high school or get the paper that morning or talk to my mom and dad.

THE TOP HALF OF THE SECOND INNING ENDS AND the Yankees come off the field and head for the dugout. I am making notes in my scorecard and checking to see who is coming to the plate for the home team. I have this vague notion that if I can find something really intriguing in a baseball sort of way, perhaps I can get my friend going here and she can begin to have as much fun as I am trying to have. It is my "dazzle her with my intimate knowledge of the nuances of the game" thing, which worked so successfully at the minor league park when we were courting. I am a little concerned that it may not be good enough for the major leagues, but it is my best shot.

Suddenly, without looking at me at all, she grabs my arm and shouts. "There it is! Look!" I look out toward center field where she is pointing, out past where Richardson and Kubek turned all of those double plays, and up over where Bernie Williams had just been patrolling center field on the same hallowed ground where Mantle and DiMaggio had roamed, up above the walls where the monuments to Ruth and Gehrig and the others are. There on the scoreboard that is shining against the night sky, I see what she has been looking for.

As a rule, I do not pay much attention to the scoreboard between innings. It is generally either full of commercials and promotions or else full of birthday greetings and such. But the shouting and the finger pointing and the grabbing of my arm has my attention.

IN THE TWILIGHT AT GREER STADIUM, MYERS CAN now see what all the rest of us saw coming a split second before. Baptist has thrown to Cruz at first to pick Myers off, and Myers has no chance to get back in time. So he does the only thing that he can do: he lights out for second in the hope that he can beat the throw from Cruz to second base.

Grinning, Nunez takes the throw from Cruz and tags Myers as he slides into second. Myers was out by ten or twelve feet. If you are a Sounds fan, it is a very nice play. If you are Myers, it is very embarrassing. He trots back to the dugout sheepishly, hoping that his manager had been looking the other way.

AT LEAST ONE OF THE UNCHANGEABLE LAWS OF THE universe is this: If you do not want it to rain, take your umbrella. It only rains when your umbrella is at home or at the office or in the car or wherever it was was when you looked at it on the way out and said to yourself, "Nah, it's not going to rain." Planning a picnic or a camping trip or to wash your car has much the same effect on rain chances.

There is a similar law in baseball. Whether you are playing or watching, if you ever turn your head during a pitch, that is the pitch that will be smashed over the wall or disappear inside the glove of the diving shortstop for the best play of the night.

Baseball is a slow, leisurely-paced affair in which not much seems to be happening and then all of a sudden it does and you can miss it if you are not very attentive. It is a game in which the ordinary happens over and over and over again for a very long time, and then suddenly something out of the ordinary happens, and sometimes even the extraordinary makes a visit. It is not a game for the impatient, perhaps.

To enjoy it, to see its beauty, one has to be willing to wait for the ordinary things to mount up, to wait for the out-of-the-ordinary to make its appearance. If you only see the highlights on television, you miss the waiting, the ordinary, the routine, the detail of the thing that makes the extraordinary just that. You diminish the extraordinary in the process.

My wife knows these things, and she made sure that I was paying attention even when I did not know that I was supposed to be. This is what the scoreboard said: THE NEW YORK YANKEES WOULD LIKE TO WELCOME ROBERT BENSON & SARA FORTENBERRY TO YANKEE STADIUM FOR THE FIRST TIME. I came right up out of my seat.

There it was, finally, my name in lights at Yankee Stadium. Not for very long, not even for as long as the few people who saw it looked at my picture in the paper all those years ago, not nearly as long as I had dreamed it would be when I thought I would be taking Mr. Richardson's place. But long enough, I guess. Long enough for me to grin and to have my breath taken away while sitting in one of the places that I had worshiped from afar.

I tipped my cap to the section all around me, who were quick to figure out what a fine gift had just been given to me. They applauded and cheered and I sat down, a little embarrassed at having been such a kid about it. But I was glad that I had not turned my head.

Never turn your head. Someday your name may be in lights, even if just for a second, and you do not want to miss it.

MAKE THE
ROUTINE PLAY

And while the premium on individual effort is never lost, eventually the marvelous communal choreography of a team almost always takes over. . . . Every assigned role on the field potentially can, and often does, change with every pitch and with each kind of pitch or each ball hit fair. The subsequent complexities and potential interactions among all the players on the field expand in incalculable ways. When in the thrall of its communal aspects, hitting, stealing, and individual initiative give way to combined playmaking, acts of sacrifice or cooperation, and obedience to signs and orders. Whether on offense or defense, the virtuoso is then subsumed into the company. The anarchic ways of solo operators are subdued by a free institution.

A. BARTLETT GIAMATTI
Baseball and the American Character

CUBS 6TH *(Sounds 4, Cubs 5)—Hatcher grounds out to Wehner at second. Zaleta grounds out to Patterson at third. Mathews lines out to Nunez behind the second-base bag for the third out. (0 runs, 0 hits, 0 errors, 0 LOB)*

SOUNDS 6TH *(Sounds 4, Cubs 5)—Patterson grounds out to Myers at second. Knorr pinch-hits for Baptist and grounds out to Ojeda at shortstop. Redman tries to bunt his way on and is thrown out by the pitcher, Norton, to end the inning. (0 runs, 0 hits, 0 errors, 0 LOB)*

IT IS SEPTEMBER AND I am trying to find a decent supper around nine o'clock on a Monday evening in a small southern town where the sidewalks were pretty much rolled up for the night about four hours ago. I spent the day driving through the hills for almost six hours in a rented car, working my way south to this little town, checking into a motel just off the town square in time for a nap and a sandwich in the coffee shop downstairs.

It used to be a Holiday Inn, I think, or at least it sure looks like it was. It has that design and architecture to it: concrete blocks and institutional colors and big windows that look out over the air conditioners to the parking lot. It has those hangers that are made so that you cannot use them if you steal them and furniture with artificial-woodgrain-finished Formica on the top.

There is not much of a dinner to be had either, though I expect that since this is a college town, there are probably some good places to go if I just knew where to look. But I am tired and do not want to get back into the car and drive anymore. I have to drive about eight hours tomorrow in order to be somewhere else and I would rather get a good night's rest than try to find a really good meal.

This is what it is like sometimes on a book tour.

IN THE SIXTH INNING AT GREER, SIX MEN COME TO the plate. Six hitters and the ball never leaves the infield. No one gets on base, and only two of them even come close. Iowa's Hatcher hits a pretty good shot toward the bag at second base, but Wehner is over to scoop it up just before it gets to the grass, and he pivots and throws Hatcher out pretty easily. Zaleta is out on a routine ground ball to Patterson at third. Nunez snares a line drive off the bat of Mathews; he ended up on his knees, but I think there was more than a little showmanship involved. I used to be a shortstop, and so I know something about these things.

In the Sounds' half, Patterson grounds out easily, as does the pinch-hitter, Knorr. Redman tries to bunt his way on, but he bunts it too hard, and it is easily fielded on a couple of hops by the pitcher and Redman is out almost before he can get out of the batter's box.

Six hitters, six routine plays, six outs. This is the way that baseball is most of the time.

THERE ARE WRITERS WHO COMPLAIN ABOUT BEING out on a book tour. I am not one of them.

The truth of the matter is that people who only write like I do, with the occasional workshop or retreat to lead somewhere, actually spend most of their lives locked in a room with a fountain pen and some blank pieces of paper and not much else, other than stacks of books to read, for company. There is a sense in which the life itself is so solitary, so far removed from the people that I hope might find my book worth reading, that it is more than a little lonely sometimes. One writes and writes and writes without ever being very certain that what one is working on will ever have any meaning to anyone but oneself. To go out and to read to people is the only way, really, to ever have any sense of whether or not one is writing something that is worth reading.

The other thing that one must say about being out on tour is that not all writers are chosen to do such a thing. Publishers of books have to make choices about how much money they are going to spend to try to sell a book that they are publishing. Very often those choices come down to whether or not the publisher believes that the book will appeal to enough people to justify the expense of sending the writer out on tour to try to find some of them. So to be chosen at all has meaning, and a writer who forgets this is approaching ungrateful, as far as I am concerned.

This night in this little town was actually a really fine thing for me. I got to read and then got to sign books for a small crowd of folks who gathered up at Square Books in Oxford, Mississippi. To be at Square Books may not mean much to some folks, but it means a lot to me.

It is one of the finest of the independent bookshops left in the country. It actually does sit right on the square in Oxford, and its windows face the courthouse. My book was in the window there, with a poster announcing the appearance. Just inside, there is a wall along the staircase that goes upstairs to the coffee bar and the porch. On the wall is a photograph of virtually every fine Southern writer who has ever lived, or so it seems. To be included in such company was a pretty good thrill.

A couple of dozen people came to the reading, and they were attentive and gracious, even though I am not nearly as well known or important a writer as they are used to having there. They asked good questions and they stood around afterward while I signed books and they were kind both to me and to my daughter, who had come along to keep me company. "Nothing flatters me more than to have it assumed that I could write prose—unless it be assumed," wrote Robert Frost, "that I once pitched baseball with distinction." I was flattered that they came to hear me read; I am flattered when anyone comes to hear me read.

It was a good night, all in all, though my daughter kept looking at me with a kind of "is this all there is?" expression on her face. I had brought her along because I did not want to travel alone—at least that was part of it. I also wanted her to see what it was like to be what I am, a writer, and all that that entails, and I was secretly hoping that I would impress her a bit along the way.

It was a routine night on a small tour for a writer whose audience is not very large. But we did our best, she and I, and did the work "that was given us to do," as the prayerbook calls it, and then we headed off to find the newspapers, to check on the pennant races, and to find something to eat. I have to confess that I do not think she was particularly impressed.

BY THE TIME THAT NASHVILLE AND IOWA HAD FINished that evening, the batters had gone to the plate 74 times. Of the 74, 51 of them had been outs.

By and large, the outs came on fairly routine plays: ground balls hit on a couple of hops to one infielder or another, easy fly balls to outfielders, a few pop-ups in the infield when someone could not get enough of the bat on the ball to drive it anywhere very hard at all. A couple of guys were forced out at one base or another when the guy behind them hit the ball weakly in the direction of an infielder who then flipped the ball to the closest base and got an out without even having to worry much about the man who had hit the ball. Fifteen times the men who came to the plate ended up striking out, and one out of three of those did not even swing at the third strike.

Of the 23 times that men got on base, nine were walks, when the pitcher could not throw enough strikes to get the batter to swing and put the ball into play. Another nine were singles, some of them sharply hit to be sure, but a couple of them of the infield variety that were hit so weakly that a routine play could not even be made on them. Almost half of the guys who got on base were left there when the third out was made.

Two of the fielders who played were in their positions for the whole game without anyone ever hitting a ball to them. Seven of the guys in the game who went to the plate never got on base.

Baseball is a game of routine things, and it is rare that something extraordinary happens. Of the 51 outs, only three or four of them came on great plays, or even above-average plays. Of the 74 times that a man went to the plate, only one in ten times was the ball hit for extra bases.

The game would last about three hours, and in those 180 minutes, something that was not routine that was caused by a hitter happened about once every twenty minutes or so. Something out of the ordinary by a fielder or a combination of fielders happened about once every half hour or so. Spine-tingling excitement was hard to come by, as far as some folks were concerned. And yet, that is baseball.

That is life too.

SOMETIMES I FIND MYSELF IN FRONT OF A GROUP OF people who want to know what it is like to be a writer. They ask questions about what a writer's life is like, and you can tell by the way that they ask the question that they want to hear that it is somehow magical and wonderful and mystical all of the time. Not many of them ever look at me and suspect that this writer's life is glamorous, but they do seem to think that it is filled with extraordinary moments somehow; that it is very unlike the lives that they lead.

"Poets are like baseball pitchers." Robert Frost again. "Both have their moments. The intervals are the tough things."

I cannot speak for other writers, though I have known a few in my life, and I have read books that some of them have written about the life of being a writer. The truth of the matter is that our lives are very routine most of the time. Maybe even more so than most folks' lives are, in fact. Most of us spend most of our days seldom seeing or talking to other people beyond those who live in the same house that we do. Most of us stay in our houses or our studios most all day and avoid the telephone and the radio. We have few visitors, certainly when we are trying to write, and we can go days or weeks without leaving our houses or our neighborhoods except to run a few errands.

Many of us have many days that are made up of little routines that we practice to get ourselves into the places and the frames of mind where we are supposed to be in order to try to make sentences. We get up at certain times, we try to show up at our writing at certain times, we work a certain number of hours or pages per day, and then we try our best to forget about the work so that we can be human beings to the people that we live with.

With the possible, and highly likely, exception that what we do very often has less material value to anyone else on earth than does the work that other people do, our lives are pretty much like everyone else's, only without the commute, the insurance benefits, or the steady paycheck.

The people who are often the most curious about what it is like to be a writer are the people who think that they want to become one. I meet those people most often when I am asked to do a workshop at a writers' conference.

They are often very interested in the mechanics of it: How many hours a day should I write? Should I use a computer or write in longhand first? Should I be in a critique group that will help me analyze my work? Is it okay to write at home on the kitchen table or do I need to have a studio to go to? They have an idea that I can give them some trick—tell them which hat to wear or what time of day that one can be sure that the writing gods will show up or some other thing—that will turn writing from routine work to glamorous occupation.

They want the answers to questions like whether or not they need an agent and how to get publishers to consider their work. They hope that I can tell them some magic thing that will take them instantly from scribbling on a legal pad at the kitchen table in the middle of the night to a review in the *New York Times* and a spot on the best-seller list.

I always disappoint them, because I do not know the answers

to those questions. And because all that I can tell them is to do the routine work: find a place to write, get up and do it every day, do it over and over and over, and do not worry about whether or not you will ever be famous or published or rich.

Annie Dillard tells the story of a young student who asked a famous writer if she thought the student might become a writer. "Do you like sentences?" asked the famous one. If one would be a writer, then one must do the routine work of writing sentences, one at a time, day after day, one sentence and then another and then another. "The page, the page will teach you to write," Dillard says.

I read somewhere that the great Honus Wagner once said, "There ain't much to being a ballplayer, if you're a ballplayer." Do you like grounders?

IN OXFORD, MY DAUGHTER AND I DISCOVERED TWO things at dinner. One was that a good dinner on the square at Oxford that night was not in the cards for us. We probably just picked the wrong place.

The other thing that we discovered was that the Braves were playing at home in Atlanta the next afternoon. Ordinarily it is not such a big deal to discover that the Braves have a home game. However, in this particular case, it was very good news indeed. Atlanta was the next stop on the tour. And not only were we headed to Atlanta, but I did not have to actually work in Atlanta until the day after that. All that I really had to do the next day was drive to Atlanta and check into the hotel. We realized that if we got up early, dark-thirty according to my daughter, and drove the six hours to Atlanta and found tickets, we could catch a Braves game. We high-fived each other, paid for our bad hamburgers, and went upstairs to pack and get some sleep.

In Atlanta the next day, we got to the ballpark and found tickets in time to see a bit of batting practice. The Braves had clinched their division a week or so before, so the crowd was small, and we ended up having a section all to ourselves. It was a little like having a private exhibition game.

When the game ended, I asked my daughter if she would like to go around to the players' entrance and see the team come out. So we did. It turned out that they were going to get on a bus and head to the airport to fly somewhere for the last three games of the regular season. So she waited along the rope line, scorecard and pen in hand, and she collected autographs like crazy. There was not much of a crowd at the game and so there was not much of a crowd along the rope line either, and she must have gotten a dozen or so. We walked back to the car with autographed shirts and baseballs and scorecards and pennants and some other stuff that I cannot recall, most of which now sits in what amounts to a small shrine on a shelf in her room. The truth is that I walked back to the car, and she sort of floated back to the car.

She would float along for two or three steps, and then she would jump out in front of me about four or five feet and hop up and down and say, "Chipper Jones" or "Bobby Cox" or "Greg Maddux," as though I had forgotten whom the Braves had put out onto the field that day. "Dad, Bobby Cox signed my shirt!" she would remind me and grin with triumph and joy. Another few steps would go by, and then, "Javy Lopez, right there," she would shout, pointing down at the scorecard. Walking down the hill toward the parking lot, it occurred to me that in the "Dad takes daughter to baseball game" category I could hardly have done any better—if not a home run, then a stand-up double at the very least.

What I did not know was that the night was about to get even better.

THERE IS A KIND OF AXIOM IN BASEBALL THAT GOES like this: If you make the routine plays 90 percent of the time, you will likely win the game 60 percent of the time. In the major leagues, a team that wins 60 percent of its games would win its division and be in contention for the playoffs every year. If they won 60 percent of the playoff games, they would most likely win the World Series too.

It is a game that from time to time is ended on a game-winning home run in the late innings, or so it seems. But if you look carefully at what happened throughout the game, you find that the late-inning heroic deed would have been of no consequence, indeed the situation that created the possibility that a big hit could win it would not have even occurred, had there not been some key moments in the game in which this player or that one either made a routine play or failed to do so.

It was true this night at Greer. In the first inning, the Sounds picked up a run when the shortstop for the Cubs could not get the ball out of his glove fast enough to turn the double play on a ground ball that should have gotten the Cubs out of the inning. Three of the Sounds' runs were scored when the Cubs' pitchers, in the ultimate failure to deliver the routine play, could not throw enough strikes and walked hitters with runners on base, moving them into scoring position.

On the other hand, the Sounds picked up a run in the second inning when two players at the plate made outs in exactly the way that they should have. Baptist, the pitcher, laid down a perfect sacrifice bunt, just the way that you are taught to do in Little League, and moved two runners up from first and second to second and third. The next hitter, Redman, hit a sacrifice fly to left that allowed Patterson to tag up and score after the catch had been made. Two routine plays, the sort that do not get much attention in the highlight films, at least not compared to the two home runs that the Cubs got in their half of the same inning, but the Sounds had picked up a run. In a game that was won by one run, those two little things made the difference.

The Cubs had more hits, more extra-base hits, and more home runs than we did. We, however, made the routine play more often and when it most needed to be made, and we won the game.

"Most baseball games are lost, not won," said Casey Stengel once. It is the routine plays, day in and day out, that make the difference in baseball, no matter how heroic one's late-inning deeds might turn out to be on occasion.

THROUGH THE KINDNESS, AND PERHAPS EVEN THE extravagance, of the fine folks at the publishing house, my daughter and I ended up that night checking into the Ritz Carlton Hotel on Peachtree Street in Atlanta. Of course it was on Peachtree; everything in Atlanta is on Peachtree Street, I think.

We went sailing into the lobby and my daughter got the full fine-hotel treatment from the minute that she walked in the door. "Good evening, Miss Benson," and "Thank you, Miss Benson" and all of that sort of thing. It was pretty heady stuff for a fourteen-year-old. It is pretty heady stuff to me too.

We had a fine dinner in the restaurant downstairs and a stroll around a few brightly lit city blocks in the evening air. We came back after our walk and sat upstairs in the lobby and listened to a piano player play songs that she liked and ate ice cream for dessert and played cards for a while. She was feeling pretty much like the princess that I keep trying to tell her that she is when we went upstairs to our room. She had a long luxurious bath and put on one of those big thick cotton robes and spread out in the middle of her very own queen-sized bed to look down at the city lights twenty stories below and sort through her Braves souvenirs while drinking orange juice from the mini-bar.

Finally it was time to go to sleep and we turned out the lights, and in the half-darkness there, with the city light creeping in, I heard her voice from the other bed. "Dad," she said, "when I grow up, I want to be a writer."

I grinned, of course. Who would not want to be a writer if this was being a writer? Even I would want to be a writer if this was all there was to it. A day at the ballpark, a big hotel, a fine meal, a bag full of treasures from your favorite team.

What I did not say, of course, was that this is not what it is like to be a writer. Being a writer is not even like being in Oxford with two dozen nice folks listening intently as though what you had written was worth hearing as it is being read. To be a writer is to spend most of your days doing routine things.

What I wanted to say was that if you want to be anything, poet or teacher or doctor or baker or candlestick maker, then the trick to it is to do the routine things that it takes to be able to do that one thing well. I know very little about what it takes to do those things, but I suspect that they are very much like the thing that I happen to do. It takes a lot of sentences to make a book, and it takes a lot of time to find them and to try to get them down on paper, just as it takes a lot of routine ground balls to make a baseball game.

But I did not say any of those things that night in Atlanta. I did not say that I think the secret to being reasonably good at whatever it is that eventually calls to you and draws you to it, whatever it is that becomes your life's work, is for you to be in love with the little things that it takes to do it. That you love to do those things over and over until you can do them every time that they need to be done, intuitively and gracefully and passionately. That there will be very few days when you will win or lose based on some heroic effort that you muster up to save the day, but there will be lots of days when it is the little things that will make all the difference.

In the category of things unsaid that night, I also resisted the temptation to give her the long list of things that I had done over the years to actually try to become a writer. I saved her from the stories about the deadlines and the rejections, the false starts and the failures, the signings where no one came to hear and the books that no one read. I did not tell her about the pages that had to be thrown away or the ideas that turned out to be only ideas and never grew up to be books. There would be time enough for that, I figured. And if I did not teach her, then the game would, if I could teach her to pay attention to it. Tonight was a night for basking in the glory of the lucky bounce that got us here to the Ritz for a brief moment.

Instead, I just said to her, "When I grow up, I want to be a writer, too."

STAND UP
AND SING

Baseball is one of the few enduring institutions in America that has been continuous and adaptable and in touch with its origins. As a result, baseball is not simply an essential part of this country; it is a living memory of what American culture at its best wishes to be. . . .

Today, in those enclosed green spaces in the middle of cities, under smoky skies, after days that weigh heavy either because of work or no work, the game reminds the people who gather at that field in the city of the best hopes and freest moments we can have.

A. BARTLETT GIAMATTI
Men of Baseball, Lend an Ear

CUBS 7TH *(Sounds 4, Cubs 5)—Garcia enters the game at pitcher for the Sounds, replacing Baptist. Johns singles. Encarnacion pops out to Wehner behind second base. Zintner bats for Norton and grounds into a 3-6-1 double play (Cruz to Nunez to Garcia) for the second and third outs. (0 runs, 1 hit, 0 errors, 0 LOB)*

SOUNDS 7TH *(Sounds 4, Cubs 5)—Ayala takes the mound for the Cubs in relief of Norton. Nunez beats out a bunt to reach first. Wehner walks, moving Nunez to second. Cruz strikes out. Laker strikes out. Brown doubles off the wall in center field, Nunez scoring from second, Wehner scoring from first. Brede strikes out to end the inning. (2 runs, 2 hits, 0 errors, 1 LOB)*

The sun is going down at Greer Stadium, and the visitors have put the leadoff man on in the top half of the seventh inning. We get Encarnacion to hit a weak pop fly to Wehner at second for the first out, and then the the Cubs send up Zintner to bat for their pitcher.

Zintner swings on the first pitch, inexplicable behavior for a pinch hitter who has not seen a pitch since batting practice a couple of hours ago, and he taps a little ground ball to the right side between first base and the mound. The Cubs were probably looking for more from him, but at least it should move the runner to second and put him into scoring position. The first baseman, Cruz, charges the ball and fields it with his bare hand while heading straight toward third base. Without breaking stride, he fires it sidearmed to second, where Nunez takes the throw and fires to first, where no one happens to be just now since it is the place that Cruz just abandoned to field the ground ball.

Baptist had come off the mound and headed straight to first as soon as he saw that Cruz was making the play on the ground ball. Running hard, keeping an eye on second base so that he can see what Nunez is doing, and occasionally dropping his glance to see where the first-base bag is, he arrives at the bag at the exact moment that the throw from Nunez does. Baptist and the ball beat the batter by a single step, executing a rare first-to-short-to-pitcher double play. (That is 3-6-1 for those of you keeping score at home.)

It is a pretty play, the sort of play that energizes a team and the fans. The home team comes off the field briskly and heads into the dugout, patting one another on the back and telling one another that it is time to get some runs. The crowd is feeling it too, so we all stand up and sing a song together.

"Take me out to the ballgame, take me out with the crowd. . . ."

BASEBALL HAS MORE THAN A FEW RITUALS AND CUS-toms that seem odd to those who are not followers of the game. And then there are some things that seem odd even to those of us who love it. But it is not really a baseball game unless they happen.

First, of course, there is the national anthem, which surely must be among the eight or ten most difficult songs to sing in all the world. I suppose that if you are going to play nine innings of the national game, then it is appropriate to sing a verse of the national song before you begin, although I have to confess that I like the game better than the song. Other countries sing songs about their countries; we sing a song about our battle flag. Then again, we are the only country on the planet whose national anthem ends with the words "Play ball." That is not altogether a bad thing, I think.

Every once in a while, you get some sort of stunning version of the song performed by some well-known performer. But those are the ones that you usually get only on television before World Series games. Generally speaking, day in and day out, the rendition is something less than overwhelming.

At Greer Stadium, most nights, a Little League team from the area has somehow ended up with the privilege of trotting out with the home team to their positions on the field before the game so that they can be on the field during the national anthem. The kids stand next to the ballplayers and solemnly place their caps over their hearts. They turn toward the flagpole in center field and stand at attention while the song is being sung. One night, the little boy who stood beside the catcher and the umpires at home plate got more into the spirit of the thing than anyone else that I can remember. During the singing of the anthem, he did a little impromptu dance in front of the plate that had those of us in the stands giggling, and the catcher and the umpires were so tickled that they could hardly stand up straight. It is the only *Star-Spangled Banner* dance that I have ever seen. It was a harbinger of things to come, too: we lost that night in a laugher, something like 17–6.

In a book called *The Education of Eismee,* I read about a kindergarten teacher in Chicago who was responsible for teaching her class the national anthem so that they could sing it for their parents at open house. She is a baseball fan and, if the book she wrote is any indication, she is considerably more entertaining than your average teacher, and so she taught them to shout "Play ball!" at the end of it. Her principal did not like it at all, a football fan probably, and she got in trouble. Later on, as she got to be a better and better teacher, she was fired. Some principals have no sense of humor. But even such un-lighthearted folks as umpires know that is the proper way to end the song.

A second of the odd little rituals is the ceremonial first pitch. Go to any baseball game, and before the thing can get under way, someone is brought out from the clubhouse where they have been hanging around with the ballplayers for a few minutes, and they are escorted to the mound to throw a pitch to the catcher behind the plate, who then trots the ball back to the mound and shakes the person's hand and stands next to him or her while someone takes a picture.

From time to time, it is a magical moment, like the time Ted Williams was rolled into the ballpark on a golf cart, tipping his hat finally, after all these years, to the fans—something he inexplicably refused to do during his great career in Boston—to throw out the first pitch at an All-Star game. The other great names of baseball, or at least a fair number of them, were there, including that year's chosen ones who were to play in the game, and they all piled onto the field around the mound to greet him and pay their respects. There was hardly a dry eye in the place, and for certain there were no dry eyes at our house.

There was the time that Yogi Berra returned to Yankee Stadium after years and years. There had been bad feelings between him and the owner of the club after Yogi had been fired as manager of the team, and Yogi had vowed not to set foot in the stadium again until the owner was gone. Finally, the owner apologized to Yogi, made his peace, and Yogi returned to the stadium for Yogi Berra Day and threw out the first ball in front of a packed house. He fired a strike, and the crowd roared. It was followed up by the Yankees' David Cone pitching a perfect game, something that has happened only a few times in the history of the major leagues.

Most of the time, though, the first pitch is thrown by someone who cannot pitch at all, and whom very few people in the stands know. It is somebody who is having a birthday or a guy who bought a hundred tickets so that his whole office could come to the game together, or a guy from the local radio station that paid for the magnetic calendars handed out that night at the gate. I have seen it done by mayors and actresses, by presidents and firemen, and by teachers and insurance salesmen.

It is pretty entertaining, though, to watch them get up on the mound and sheepishly try to fire the thing home. It looks closer on television. More often than not, the ball bounces up to the plate on two hops and the catcher picks it up. It is exciting to the one who threw it, but to the rest of us, it is just funny. But the game cannot actually begin until it is done.

Finally, there is the seventh-inning stretch. It is not so funny that people would feel the need to stand up and stretch after sitting in their seats for an hour and a half, but if the truth is told, not many of them have been sitting there the whole time. People are forever milling around at a ball game. It reminds me of an anthill sometimes. I read somewhere that if you walk a golf course during a round of golf, as opposed to riding in a golf cart, you cover about six miles. I have seen people walk that far at a baseball game before, I believe. Most of them, I have observed, have seats in the middle of the row that I am sitting in.

What is funny about the stretch is that we all stand up and sing together. We do not know each other, by and large. Some of us have had more than our share of trouble that day and do not feel much like singing at all. But when the time comes we stand up and sing.

AS A CARD-CARRYING MEMBER OF THE SECRET SOCI-ety of Very Shy Persons, an organization that you may not have heard of for obvious reasons, I am not one for public displays of much of anything at all, even at the ballpark. I am a polite-but-sustained-applause sort of guy. I would take issue with the word bland, but I would rather be that than boorish. I am not the sort of person who is likely to stand up and sing in public.

So I was more than a little surprised at myself when, in the summer that I was courting my wife at Greer Stadium, I suddenly developed the overwhelming need to sing along with the crowd during the seventh-inning stretch. I was discovering a lot of things that summer, about myself, and about her, and about what ultimately became us.

There are generally only two times when I can be persuaded to sing in public, alhough I must confess that I am not called upon very often to do it, and rightly so.

One of those times is when I am sitting in the first pew at the cathedral where I worship. The singing is part and parcel of my oblation and I am expected to participate as fully as I can, whether that particular part of my worship sounds very good or not. Fortunately, there are plenty of good singers in the cathedral, and I make sure to sit in their general vicinity so that I sound pretty good, even though I never sing loudly enough to get in their way or to be heard over them.

The other time that I am willing to sing is in the middle of the seventh inning at the ballpark. (I have not yet progressed to singing the national anthem, though I do remove my hat and hum, "dum ta-dum dum dum dum," just before the others sing, "Oh, say does that star-spangled banner yet wave . . .")

But when the seventh inning comes, there I am. "Take me out to the ballgame, take me out with the crowd . . ."

Everyone knows the song, of course. Even people who do not know baseball or even care to know baseball know the song. And there are those of us who can even remember the day that we actually fell in love with the song.

IT IS FALL, AND IT IS COLD AND GRAY IN CHICAGO. I have just moved to the city, yesterday actually, and in a couple of days I will be alone here in this city. In some ways, I will be alone for the first time in my whole life. I have always lived near home, and around my family pretty much, and it seems strange to me to be in this place with only one person that I know.

The brother who has driven up from Tennessee with me to help me move my things is one of my two younger brothers, much younger actually. When I left home to go to college, he had not yet even started school. We used to joke that we grew up in different families together. This trip with him is the first thing that I can remember doing that involved just the two of us. It would not be the last. As the years went by and we both grew older, we both ended up with divorces and children, children that we tried to be fathers to in houses where our children did not live every day, and we tried to be friends to each other. His children are the same ages and the same genders as mine, and so the six of us do a lot of things together.

So I take my brother to see the Cubs play. I love the game, and the park is not too far from the studio apartment that we have just unloaded my small amount of stuff in, and I have never been to Wrigley Field. My brother does not particularly care for the game, but I am trying to say thanks for the help and to show him some sort of big-city thing that he has never seen, and so we go to the game.

There is not much of a crowd that day; the Cubs have long been out of the pennant race, for decades I learn later, and it is a day game on a weekday, and the stands are pretty empty. It does not matter much to me; I am sitting in the most beautiful ballpark of all, and I have nowhere that I am supposed to be for a couple more days yet.

When I was young, maybe eight or nine, my father took me to a ball game in Cleveland. It was a rainy night in the late spring, I think, and the Indians were playing the Yankees. It was in the old Cleveland ballpark, and I remember very little about it. But I would have seen the immortals that night—Maris and Mantle and Richardson and Berra and the rest. In the summer when I was twelve, I visited my aunt who lived in Cincinnati, and she took me to see the Reds play. But for many years, until that afternoon with my brother, my major league experience was limited to the Game of the Week and the World Series, both on television. And on television, the seventh-inning stretch is simply another commercial break.

The seventh inning comes around at Wrigley that day and the visitors bat and the side is retired. The Cubs head in to take their turn at the plate and the crowd stands up to stretch. To tell the truth, since it has been close to thirty years since I had been at a professional ballpark, I had forgotten about the stretch.

"Are you ready?" booms a big voice out over the stadium. "Are you ready?" That is when Harry Caray taught me one of the finer points of the game. And that is when I fell in love with the song.

HARRY CARAY WAS THE VOICE OF THE CHICAGO CUBS, a legendary broadcaster who had been the voice of the St. Louis Cardinals for years before he came to Chicago. He did radio broadcasts during the days before television, and later managed to make the jump into televised baseball work. I learned more about him later and about his long career with Cardinals, but on this day—this first day, so to speak—I did not even know who he was.

The broadcast booth at Wrigley Field hangs down from the bottom of the upper deck and just sort of hovers in the space behind home plate. If you are in a field box, you can see into the windows of the booth if you turn around in your seat. Harry and his broadcast partners would sit at a table and do both the radio and the television coverage at the same time. He would work the television broadcast for a few innings and then swap off and do radio for a while, so that fans in the hinterlands who could only follow the team on the radio would still get to hear him. "My whole philosophy," he used to say, "is to broadcast the game the way a fan would broadcast it."

As the years went by, Harry became a larger-than-life baseball person, a sort of unofficial ambassador and representative of Every Fan. Most baseball fans recognized his great shock of white hair pulled back from around his wide face. He wore these big black horn-rimmed glasses, and spoke in a growly sort of voice, the sort of voice that you might expect to hear if a friendly grizzly bear had become a baseball announcer. He invented phrases that worked their way into the baseball lexicon. "The friendly confines of Wrigley Field," he used to call the ballpark, and as I've told you, "It could be, it might be, it is . . . a home run" was his famous home-run call. He has a restaurant that caters to the sporting crowd, and he is recognized and loved everywhere. I bought a baseball hat at Wrigley once with a caricature of him on it, and it is one of my proudest possessions.

But on that first afternoon at Wrigley, I had never seen Harry before. And so I had never seen Harry do what Harry did next. "Are you ready?" he shouts down to the crowd below. They shout back that they are. "Are you ready?" he shouts again, just to be sure. The affirmative response is louder this time, and by then everyone has turned to face him.

"A-one, a-two, and a-three," he shouts as he leans out of the broadcast booth, through the open window that hangs in the air there above home plate. "Take me out . . ." he begins, and the crowd joins in. They sort of hurry and get in quick, too, right after the word "Take," because Harry went 0-for-life in the tune-carrying department, though nobody much cared. It was okay to sing along with Harry, but you did not want him to go solo.

"For it's one, two, three strikes you're out," we sing, "at the old ball game." The crowd roars, or at least makes what such a small number of us can muster up in the roar department. "Now, let's get some runs!" Harry shouts above the cheers, which is his own way to end the song, and now it is mine, too.

On another afternoon, years later, my wife made her first trip to Wrigley Field. We sat in the sunshine on a glorious day in May and the Braves were in town to go up against the young phenom for the Cubs, Kerry Wood, and the ivy on the walls was blowing gently in the breeze. We sat in the lower field boxes, only about six rows or so off the brick wall that borders the field. We were so close to the field, she claimed that she could hit the home-plate umpire with a thrown program if it became necessary.

The middle of the seventh inning came and everyone stood up, and turned to look in Harry's direction. And he leaned out of the window almost right above us and the crowd began to cheer. "A-one, a-two, and a-three"—and she turned to me with tears in her eyes. I do not know exactly why she did that, but it seemed entirely appropriate to me, and it has only grown to be more so as the years have passed.

So we sang, both of us shy people, right along with Harry, joining our voices with the faithful in the friendly confines. Watching Harry lead that song, and hearing all of those people sing it, one of whom I dearly love, was one of the sweetest things in the world.

THE STORY IS THAT IT WAS PRESIDENT WILLIAM Howard Taft who accidentally began the custom of the seventh-inning stretch.

In 1910, the President made his way from the White House across town for a game between the Washington Senators and the Philadelphia Athletics. It turns out that he had been a pitcher in the sandlots in Cincinnati when he was young. One day in his twenties he had been pounded unmercifully off the mound by an opponent, and, one supposes, into politics, and had sworn off being on the mound ever since. On this day, he threw out what was the first presidential ceremonial first pitch in the major leagues. He kept his promise to stay off the mound, however, by throwing it to the catcher from his box seat.

Mr. Taft was a large man, three hundred pounds' worth of large man, and the story is that during the middle of the seventh inning he rose to stretch himself, having been crammed into a seat for quite a while. Fans, noticing that in the front row the President of these United States had stood up, respectfully did the same, thereby starting, as George Will observed, "a useful tradition, which is more than can be said for most Presidents."

THERE IS NO PRESIDENT ON HAND TO RISE UP AND start the stretch at Greer, and there is no Harry Caray to lead the song. In fact, this season the folks at Greer have inaugurated a custom of having a Little League team lead us in the song. They seldom can sing it, or even remember the words for that matter, so the rest of us have trouble following along and the thing falls flat most times. But when the song has wandered its way to its conclusion, I pretend that we actually sang it and then on behalf of Harry, and to no one in particular, I say, "Now, let's get some runs." We can use some tonight, we are down 5 to 4, and we only have nine outs left to work with.

And the home team obliges. Nunez, Wehner, and Cruz—the heart of the order—are due up in the seventh.

Iowa's left-handed pitcher is replaced by the right-hander Ayala. Which means that Nunez, who is a switch-hitter, will bat left-handed now instead of right-handed. Two things are true about that setup. One is that Nunez is three steps closer to first, which means that he has a better chance to use his speed to get on base. The second is that when Ayala follows through on his throw to the plate, he falls toward first. As the first pitch from Ayala leaves his hand, Nunez squares up and lays a perfect bunt between third base and the mound. The only guy who has a play is Ayala, and he is falling the wrong way, looking back over his right shoulder as the ball rolls to a complete stop beside the mound. By the time he picks it up, Nunez is only two steps from first, and Ayala is in trouble. The leadoff hitter is on.

A walk given up to Wehner moves Nunez to second. The next two hitters strike out, and the count goes to 3-2 on Brown. With two out and the count full, the runners are moving on the pitch and Brown doubles off the wall in right field. Both Nunez and Wehner score easily—6 to 5 for the home team.

HARRY PASSED AWAY, A COUPLE OF SPRINGS AGO now, just before opening day, as I recall. Baseball was his life. He used to say, "Now, you tell me, if I have a day off during the baseball season, where do you think I'll spend it? The ballpark. I still love it; always have, always will." He has lots of days off now, and I bet he is at a game somewhere.

If you go to a Cubs game now, there is always a person who leans out the window at the seventh-inning stretch to lead the crowd in the song, in honor of Harry. They ask the crowd if they are ready, just like Harry did, and they count it down, just like Harry did, and they do it with all of the fun and energy that they can muster. And the crowd looks up to the booth where Harry used to be standing above them and waves and cheers at the celebrity—the athlete or movie star or singer or political personage—who has been chosen to fill Harry's shoes for the day. The substitutes always know that they cannot fill those shoes, but they do their best and the fans are generally kind to them. I imagine that most folks in the ballpark still turn around from time to time and expect to see Harry there. It is what happens when those that you love are gone from their familiar places.

The brother who helped me move to Chicago and went with me to Wrigley for the first time on that chilly September afternoon passed away the same spring. Baseball was not his life; indeed, if one was to talk about things in those terms, earth was his life. He was a landscaper, and his only real connection to the sport was accidental—his game began in the spring and ended each year in the fall, just like baseball. In the early spring, when the boys of summer were at spring training, he was getting ready for summer too, checking his equipment and lining up clients and pulling off winter mulch and checking out the nurseries to buy plants.

In my "half" of the family—where we older two of the four brothers grew up—we played baseball when we were young. For one reason or another, the two younger brothers did not. This brother never did become much of a baseball fan. I know for a fact that he did not even know the words to the song that day that he and I first heard Harry lead it. I do not know if he ever learned them. But I can still see the two of us, in my memory, about three rows off the wall, down along the right-field line, maybe thirty or forty feet past first base. And I can see us laughing together at the game and the people and the song and whatever else it was that made us laugh together that day.

If I look closely at my memory, I can see the anxiety beneath the smile on my face, my fear and unease at being away from home and everyone and everything that I loved and knew. And because I now know all of the things that were to happen to me in the couple of years that I lived in Chicago, and the years that came after them and were so much changed by those two years, I am a little saddened by the picture of me that my memory holds.

My brother is simply standing there, beside me—tall, good-looking, with a big grin on his face. In his face I can see no hint of the things that were killing him even then, the things none of us, even he, knew about at the time. He was so young and so pretty and so funny. "There are some men too gentle to live among wolves," wrote the poet James Kavanaugh, and it turned out that my brother was one of them. Life is not always easy for any of us, and for some of us it can be more than can be borne. That was what happened to my brother in the end.

I heard that on opening day of the baseball season that began after Harry died, when it came time for the seventh-inning stretch, the crowd stood up and looked toward the booth behind home plate in Wrigley Field and that Harry's widow led the crowd in singing the song. I wish that I had been there for that. It must have been something like an anthem, I suspect—if not the national one then maybe something like the ones that you sing in church sometimes.

By that same opening day, my brother was gone. If he had been around still, he would not even have known that it was opening day anyway, though before the spring was over, he and his kids would have come to the ballpark with me and my kids at least once or twice. And we would have laughed at him grinning at us when we stood up to sing the song, a good-natured laugh, the kind that he laughed when he caught you doing something silly, and then he would have followed it up with a smile and a hug, and a "Luv ya, buddy."

When we gathered up in the church to say our goodbyes to him, we sent him out to wherever he is now with an anthem more suited to him. "All creatures of our God and King . . ." we sang as they carried him up the aisle and out into the spring and away from us for all seasons to come. It was hard to let him go. It was good to have a song to sing as he left.

And it is good to be reminded from time to time, on your average Thursday when life is not necessarily so great, that sometimes there is just nothing for it but to stand up and sing.

SLIDE, SID, SLIDE

Never was a game better matched to its season, or better, never was a season—from spring to early autumn—better matched by a game. The game was outdoors, on grass, in the sun. It began at winter's end, and ended before frost. It made the most of high skies, clement weather, and the times of planting and growth. Until the advent of lights, then domed stadia and artificial turf, baseball was earthbound in the sense of using the earth and climate to advantage and the rhythms of light, shadow, and dusk and spring, summer, and early fall as part of itself. To be earthbound in such a fashion is, to me, pure heaven.

A. BARTLETT GIAMATTI
Baseball and the American Character

CUBS 8TH *(Sounds 6, Cubs 5)—Myers is called out on strikes. Ojeda doubles into the gap in right center to Brown. Gonzalez walks. Clontz relieves Garcia on the mound (double switch: Clontz for Brede in the seventh spot in the batting order, Brinkley for Garcia in the ninth spot). Hatcher is called out on strikes. Zaleta strikes out for the third out. (0 runs, 1 hit, 0 errors, 2 LOB)*

SOUNDS 8TH *(Sounds 6, Cubs 5)—Patterson grounds out to the pitcher Ayala. Zosky bats for Brinkley and strikes out. Redman fouls out to Encarnacion on the third-base side to end the inning. (0 runs, 0 hits, 0 errors, 0 LOB)*

THERE IS A COSMIC TRUTH when it comes to kids and baseball diamonds and sliding in the dirt that is akin to the more generally known cosmic truth about little kids and mud puddles. Most everyone knows that if a kid sees a puddle, the kid has to jump in it and splash the water. The cosmic necessity of the jump is increased exponentially by the cleanliness of the clothes and the gravity of the event to which everyone is headed. If you are going to church, the splash, and therefore the signs of the splash, must be larger. If you are going to Grandmother's for dinner, then the size of the splash needs to go up or down according to how many other relatives will be present, including the aunts who believe that you are not fit to be a parent anyway because your kids are always too rowdy. Regardless of what parents think, this behavior is not calculated; neither is it thought through at the moment so that a child has a chance to weigh the deed and its consequences and make a choice. It is instinct, pure and simple and joyous.

Those who do not frequent baseball diamonds do not know about the cosmic principle known as If They See It, They Will Slide. If you are a kid, and you are running toward a base on a baseball diamond, and there is absolutely no reason to slide, you will slide anyway. Just for the joy of it. Just for the pretend of it. Just for the dust and the dirt of it. Just for the fact that some cosmic force requires it. It may well be how, if not exactly why, the game of baseball was invented in the first place.

IN THE TOP OF THE EIGHTH AT GREER, OJEDA COMES to the plate for Iowa with one out and nobody on, his team in need of base runners to overcome the one-run lead that the Sounds currently hold. He bats second in the order and knows that his job is to get on base, try to get himself into scoring position somehow, and hope that one of the next three hitters, the club's big hitters, can drive him home to tie the game. There will not be many more chances for him or for the Cubs—they only have six outs left.

Ojeda is not a big guy; most middle infielders are small guys, in fact. He is the sort of player who has quick hands and feet, can get a glove on almost anything hit in his direction, and has a good arm. He is probably on this team for the same reason that he has always been on any team—his glove, not his bat. For a player like Ojeda, and there are lots of them, the hope is that he can scratch and claw his way on base any way that he can—a walk, an error, a slow-rolling ground ball, a bunt, anything. There are other guys who can do more with the bat than he can and are generally the ones counted on to get the big base hits. His job is to be on base when they do, so that he can use his speed to score. So far this evening, he has not been on base.

Ojeda slaps a soft line drive into the gap in right center field, and as he makes his turn at first, the ball has sort of died after hitting the base of the wall. The ball should have bounced twenty or thirty feet back toward the right fielder but it did not, and as Brown retrieves it and turns to fire the ball to second base, Ojeda is maybe thirty feet away from the bag and it is clear that he will be safe at second with no play, a stand-up double.

So, of course, Ojeda slides into second. It is a beautiful head-first slide that is absolutely perfect and positively unnecessary. He does it, I think, for the pure joy of it. The manager probably mutters under his breath at the way that it showed up the other team. The trainer fumes because that is a good way to get hurt and if you do not have to slide then you should not. Somewhere in Mexico his mother groans at the thought of how many dirty uniforms she had to wash when he was growing up. Nunez, whom I have seen do the same thing, takes the throw from the right fielder and looks down at Ojeda hugging the second-base bag at his feet and just grins at him.

"Remember, fans," booms out the Greer public-address announcer, "following tonight's game, all kids under the age of sixteen will be running the bases. . . ." He goes on to give instructions as to where to line up to enter the field and so on. I am always a little disappointed when he makes the announcement; it means that the game will actually end sometime, and I am generally hoping that it will last forever.

They gather the kids up under the 327 sign in left field, right where the left-field foul line intersects with the left-field fence. They line up in a long line, a couple of hundred kids or so, and march down the left-field line behind the mascot. There are some parents here and there, holding the hands of those who are very young and intimidated by the field and the crowd. They will only be that way this once; they must be rookies. The next time around, they will be seasoned veterans and they will motion for their parents to just wait for them over by the first-base dugout, because their hand-holding services will no longer be needed, at least not for running the bases at the ballpark.

There are a couple of ushers at home plate, and they send the kids off in some sort of haphazard order, doing their best to get the kids to go one at a time, and trying to time it so that the little kids do not get run over by the big kids. Once they get out onto the base paths, the line sort of stretches out and there is enough room for the big kids to go around the little kids and it all works out. But right around home plate, with all these kids lining up and taking off toward first and coming in to home plate, it is a little confusing. From time to time, one of the kids, against the rules that were given to him as he took off toward first, will slide into home when he or she comes around. Every once in a while there will be a kid who slides into second and third as well.

My son slid into home and nearly took out a couple of big kids after a Sounds game once. The ushers were unhappy with him, but I thought it was a pretty good slide myself.

ON ONE SUMMER NIGHT, WE TOOK MY SON TO THE ballpark when he was very small. He must have been only four or five years old. You could always pretty much count on him to be tired out by the fifth inning or so in those days; being a kid can be exhausting work, especially during the summer. There were some nights that he would be ready to head for the house long before the rest of us were.

If he was not tired before we went, he would be after three innings or so because he would have spent pretty much the entire time walking the ballpark. In those days, he and his older sister subscribed to the theory that one had to eat something different after the top half of every inning and go find some collectible treasure of some sort after the bottom half of every inning. From time to time I would gently remind them that there was a baseball game being played on the field down there below us. They would look at me as though I did not understand that the game was just something to keep parents occupied while their kids wandered around.

Along about the sixth inning one night, after my son had collected everything that he could collect and eaten everything that he could eat, having exhausted the meager amount of money that I had in my right-hand pocket, he got tired and crawled up into my lap. (Never put all of your money in one pocket at the ball game. That way you can still have some when you get ready to take your kids home.) I was happy to have him there, and if the truth be told I still am, though he is a young man now and it does not happen very often. I was also happy to be able to watch the last few innings in some measure of peace and contentment. That, of course, is when the rain came.

It was a little summer squall, the kind that pops up quickly and sends down sheets of rain for fifteen or twenty minutes and then disappears just as quickly. The umpire threw up his hands and announced that he was suspending play to wait out the rain. The players ran off the field to the dugouts. The fans who were sitting out in the parts of the ballpark where there was no roof over their heads ran for the exits to get back up under the stadium where the concourses can keep you dry and the concession stands can take your money. We sat where we were because, in my infinite wisdom, I had purchased tickets for seats that were just up under the lip of the stadium roof in case the rain came. I hate milling around in the concourses. It is too crowded and you end up spending about eighty-four cents per minute per person to stand there.

Suddenly my son sat up and started shouting, "Dad, look down on the field." He was wide awake now, and not nearly as ready to go home as he had been only moments before. For the first time all night he was interested in something that was going on down on the field. There were about fifteen guys from the grounds crew rolling the tarp out onto the field to protect the infield from the rain so that it would be playable after the rain delay.

Once the tarp had been wrestled onto the field and the infield had been covered, the grounds crew beat a hasty retreat into the dugouts that the players had abandoned for the clubhouse. After a few minutes, the Rain Man appeared. He was one of the grounds crew, and he came up out of the first-base dugout and stood in the rain in the on-deck circle for a few minutes and took a few imaginary swings with an imaginary bat. As he made his way to the plate, he motioned for the crowd to cheer and so we did.

Rain Man stood in at approximately the right-handed batter's box and took a couple of pitches. We know that he did because he would get into his stance and stare out toward the mound and then whip his head around as the "pitch" went by him. Then he would back out of the box and tap his cleats with his bat, so to speak, and then dig back in for the next pitch.

He "swung" at the next pitch and lined it into the gap in left and took off running at full speed, splashing the huge puddles that had begun to settle onto the tarp. Or at least I think that is where the ball went because of the way that he turned his head as he rounded first and headed for second. About fifteen feet from second, he threw his hands out in front of him and executed a near-perfect, headfirst slide into second. The slide itself was perfect; the near part is that he kept sliding until he had slid past the base and then past shortstop and then past the tarp and then about fifteen feet out onto the left-field grass. The crowd stood and cheered as he raised his hand to call time the way you do after you slide, and then he got up and trotted back to the bag.

The imaginary hitter who came up next must have had a base hit, because Rain Man paused for a moment and looked to right field, as if waiting to see if the ball was going to drop. When it was clear to him that it was, he took off for third, slowing a little as he made the turn and headed for home. A few seconds and another headfirst slide later, Rain Man slid into the wall behind home plate, after having cleared the edge of the tarp and plowed through a patch of mud on the way. Dizzy Dean would have said that he "slud into home." When someone asked him about his trademark word, he said, "Slud is something more than slid. It means sliding with great effort."

Rain man stood up, drenched and mud-covered, but safe at home, by a mile I guess. And then he tipped his cap and disappeared into the dugout.

It was my son's favorite play of the night, maybe of all time, and he stood in front of me, transfixed. For the rest of the summer, every time we would go through the gate to the ballpark, he would ask me if I thought we would get to see them cover the field that night. Sadly, though the rain came again some nights, the Rain Man never came to bat again.

I LEARNED MY SLIDING SKILLS AT A PLACE CALLED Shelby Park in East Nashville. My father used to take us there to watch the softball games during the summer. The church that we attended had two teams, or at least two that I remember, and a lot of his friends played on the teams, guys that he had grown up with and other people whom we knew from the church. He told me that he used to play with them, back when he was a school-boy. By his own admission, he was generally the last one chosen, and if he did get into the game it was always in right field, home of the poor fielders.

He had moved away from town in the early fifties, and was gone for ten years or so, first to attend college and seminary, then to pastor in a series of small churches in different parts of the country. When we moved back to Nashville, he would go and watch the games, probably as a way to reestablish his connections with his old friends. My memory is that we all went to see the games quite a bit, including my mother. There were always families there to watch their husbands and fathers and brothers play, and it must have been part and parcel of the social world of the people in our church in the summertime. The park was not far from where we lived at the time, or from where most of those friends of my father's lived either. A couple of years later, we moved north to the country outside of town, and my Shelby Park days were over.

My father played a little golf when he was younger, but I remember seeing him with a club in his hands only one time. He hit golf balls and baseballs left-handed, and he was trying to teach me to hit a golf ball left-handed. I am right-handed and it did not go too well. My mother said that one day he had been out playing golf with his friends and came home early from the course and put his clubs away and never took them out again. He was enough of a competitor to learn to hate losing but not enough of a golfer to learn how to beat his friends on the course.

He played tennis in college, in California. He was on his college team, and I always figured that if you could make a college tennis team in California you must be able to play. It was his favorite game to play; he even had a tennis court put in at our house, and when I was in high school we spent many nights playing there after supper. He was not very strong physically ever in his life, and through most of those years he was ill and never had much strength or stamina. He used to complain about his old rag arm after almost every serve.

My brother and I would go with him to Shelby Park, but we did not go to watch the games, we went to play in the dirt. When a game would end, we would run the bases, over and over, sliding at each one and pretending that the throw was on its way and that we were bringing home the winning run every time. When it was time for the next game to start, and there were usually two or three games on each of the four diamonds every night, we would move to the next one that was vacant and run and slide some more.

When I was playing Little League baseball, I learned pretty quickly that if your uniform was not dirty when you headed for the house, then you probably had not slid, and if you had not slid then you were probably not on base, and if you were not on base, then you did not have a very good game, and so to be sure that I at least looked like I had had a good game I would slide into a base at the earliest opportunity just in case I did not get a chance to later. There was nothing worse than going home from the ballpark with a clean uniform. I was not taught this—by my ball-playing father or anyone else, for that matter—I knew it instinctively. The way all ballplayers do.

IT IS THE FALL OF 1992 AND THE ATLANTA BRAVES are in the ninth inning of the seventh game of the National League Championship Series. They are down by two runs to the Pirates, who forced them to seven games in the playoffs the year before. For the first time in a long time, it seems as though everyone that I know is watching a baseball game on television.

For years here in the South, we had no major league baseball at all. Then in the latter part of the century, as the major leagues expanded, we began to get teams here and there, but for a long time it was only Houston and Atlanta. The Braves were not very good at all for a long time, and then suddenly, or so it seemed, they were in the Series in the 1990s. I think it was at least partly because they were a Southern team that it seemed like people all over our town were cheering for them and following them daily as the season drew to its close.

Atlanta loads the bases in the ninth, and then they pick up a run on a pop fly when the runner tags up on the catch and scores from third. Then the Pirate reliever walks the next batter to load the bases again. David Justice is on third base for the Braves and Sid Bream is on second, and the Braves need one run to tie and two runs to win. Francisco Cabrera comes on to pinch-hit for the

Braves. The tension is pretty high in the stands in Atlanta, and it is pretty high at my house too.

Cabrera laces a sharp single into short left field and the runners start to move. Justice scores easily and the game is tied. Bream takes off from second toward third, and when he arrives, he is greeted by the sight of the third-base coach, who is waving him home as though Sid can actually run. As Sid makes his turn and heads for the plate, all Braves fans everywhere collectively hold their breath and begin to wonder why in the world he is being waved home. To this day, there are Braves fans who cannot get over the fact that Sid was not replaced on second by a pinch runner long before Cabrera hit the short single to left.

Sid is not a fast runner. Sid is not even a fast walker. He is a big man who plays first base and was picked up at the beginning of the season to drive in other people, people who can actually run. "I ain't no athlete, lady," said Phillies first baseman John Kruk to a reporter once, "I'm a ballplayer." Sid Bream could have said the same thing about himself. He has been hampered by injuries to his back and legs all season, and the injuries have made him even slower than he usually is.

When Sid makes his turn, he is going full speed and there is no Brave fan on earth who believes that full speed according to Sid Bream is going to get him home safely with the winning run.

THERE ARE ALL KINDS OF THEORIES AS TO WHY BASE-ball occupies such a revered place in our national psyche. One of them that I think may be true is that we have all played it in some form or fashion at one time or another.

To some degree, we have all played the game in the backyards in our neighborhoods when were growing up, or on the playgrounds a little bit when we were in school. At the very least we played kickball, its derivative form. We have all taken a turn at bat and we have all tried to knock it where someone was not so that we could get on base. We have all been tagged out at some time in our lives, and we have scored a run a time or two in our lives, and we have come across the plate with the winning run maybe a time or two as well.

A fair number of us have never tried to run the ball for a touchdown or raced up and the down the basketball court, but nearly all of us have played baseball somewhere. That is why there is something familiar to us every time that a batter steps to the plate to try to hit the ball, and every time that a fielder tries to make a play on a ball hit hard in his direction, and every time that a runner tries to beat a throw to a base. We know what that feels like in some small way, no matter at what level we played. There is something in us that knows the basic elements of the game at some remembered level. We may not have done much more than have played once or twice a year when we were young at a church retreat or a family reunion. We may have only played in Little League and then never again. We may have played on recreational softball teams. But we all somehow know what it feels like to turn the corner at third and head for home, carrying a whole team's hopes along with us.

SID BREAM STEAMS AROUND THIRD AND HEADS FOR the plate as the left fielder fields the ball cleanly and comes up throwing, throwing a strike to home plate to be exact. It is no mean feat to do that in such a situation, and we all watch the ball come flying toward the plate on a line, straight and true, racing Sid to home.

Justice has touched the plate and retreated about ten to fifteen feet away and is waving with both hands for Sid to slide. The umpire has taken off his mask and tucked it under his arm, and has moved out a few feet in front of home plate in order to be able to call the play that is about to be made. The pitcher is about halfway between the mound and third base, facing the left fielder and holding his arms up to guide the throw. In some situations the pitcher will cut off the throw if there is no chance to get the runner, but on this day there will be no cutoff because if the run scores then the season is over. The third-base coach for the Braves is standing in his coach's box, making a big circle with his right arm, the one that means keep going and do not stop until you get home, and has turned toward the plate a little bit now and you can read his lips and he is shouting what all of us are shouting—"Slide, Sid, slide!"—as if Sid Bream, who grew up dreaming of a moment just like this, did not know what to do.

Slide he does, and the umpire calls him safe and Sid lies back on his back in the dust and begins to laugh. His teammates pile on top of him in celebration. On this day Sid has slud in safe at home and brought a whole lot of the rest of us home with him.

EVERY LITTLE KID WHO HAS EVER PLAYED THE game, who has ever run the bases at the softball park or the Little League diamond or the minor league park after the game, has dreamed of just such a moment. It is the bottom of the ninth and it is up to you to come home with the winning run. It is a race between you and the ball. You make your turn around third and head for home for all you are worth, and the sound of your feet and of the cheers and of your chest heaving are all that you can hear. You see very little—the base path, the catcher, the plate—there is no time for anything else and nothing else that matters anyway.

No one has to tell you to slide, it is the only way to bring home the winning run. It is the stuff of dreams, it is, and you have known all along that if you got the chance you could make one come true. You only have to be willing to throw yourself through the air and be covered in the dirt and dust and glory that signifies that you played hard today and held back nothing at all.

THE BEST GAME EVER

Baseball is quintessentially American in the way that it tells us that much as you travel and far as you go, out to the green frontier, the purpose is to get back home, back to where the others are . . . that you may leave home but if you forget where home is, you are truly lost and without hope.

A. BARTLETT GIAMATTI
Men of Baseball, Lend an Ear

CUBS 9TH *(Sounds 6, Cubs 5)—Mathews is called out on strikes. Johns grounds out to Patterson at third. Wallace is brought in to pitch for Clontz. Encarnacion singles and moves up to second on a wild pitch. Liniak pinch-hits for Ayala and draws a walk. Myers takes the count full and is called out on strikes to end the game. (0 runs, 1 hit, 0 errors, 2 LOB)*

SOUNDS 9TH *(Sounds 6, Cubs 5)—Did not bat.*

Final score: Nashville 6, Iowa 5.

Iowa Cubs	030	200	000—5
Nashville Sounds	121	000	20x—6

Winning Pitcher: Garcia (SV—Wallace). Losing Pitcher: Ayala.

DP—Nashville 1 (Cruz, Nunez and Baptist). PO—Myers picked off by Baptist in the 5th. CS—0. E—0. BB—Off Norton 5 (Nunez, Wehner, Patterson, Nunez, Wehner); Off Ayala 1 (Wehner); Off Baptist 1 (Hatcher); Off Garcia 1 (Gonzalez); Off Wallace 1 (Liniak). GIDP—Zintner. HR—(4) Hatcher off Baptist in the 2nd, 0 on; Zaleta off Baptist in the 2nd, 0 on; Laker off Norton in the 3rd, 0 on; Mathews off Baptist in the 4th, 0 on. LOB—Iowa 3, Nashville 7. RBI—Hatcher 1, Zaleta 1, Johns 1, Mathews 2; Laker 2, Redman 1, Wehner 1, Brown 2. RUNS SCORED—Hatcher 1, Zaleta 2, Johns 1, Mathews 1; Nunez 2, Brede 1, Patterson 1, Laker 1, Wehner 1. SAC—Baptist 1, sacrifice bunt in the 2nd; Redman 1, sacrifice fly in the 2nd. SO—By Norton 3 (Brown, Cruz, Cruz); by Ayala 3 (Cruz, Laker, Brede); by Baptist 4 (Encarnacion, Myers, Hatcher, Ojeda); by Garcia 1 (Myers); by Clontz 3 (Hatcher, Zaleta, Mathews); by Wallace 1 (Myers). SB—0.

IF YOU GO TO THE MAJOR League Baseball scoreboard page on the Internet, which is, by my reckoning, as good a reason as any for actually having access to the Internet, you can check the scores and stories from yesterday's games in the early-morning hours well before the newspaper man shows up in your neighborhood. The box scores are actually my own real reason for picking up the newspaper too, now that I come to think of it. "Baseball as scripture," Mr. Giamatti saith once. Amen.

After you have checked the scores and the standings, and checked on how your favorite players did last night, and checked to be sure that no one that you follow closely got hurt or traded or shipped back down to the minors, and if you have some time to kill before you have to begin your day, you can wander your way to the Baseball History pages. I know this because I did just that the other morning.

I was looking to see what happened in baseball on April 17, 1952, the day that I was born. There was no reason for my looking it up; I was just curious. I was probably trying to avoid having to begin to try to write sentences. Being a writer is a little like being a ballplayer. Some days you win, some days you lose, and some days you get rained out. If you feel a rainout coming on, you fool around on the Internet. It keeps you sitting at the computer so that it looks like you are working, and you can tell yourself, and anyone who asks, that you spent the morning at your desk doing research.

Nothing major actually happened in the majors on the day that I was born. An umpire named Bill Summers fined seven ballplayers from the Indians and the White Sox for fraternizing before a game, whatever that means. It must not have meant much—the fine was only five dollars each.

The day of my first birthday, though, Mickey Mantle did hit a 555-foot home run in the old Griffith Park in Washington, D.C. On my twelfth birthday the major baseball news of the day was that the Mets lost to the Pirates 4–3 in the first game played at Shea Stadium. The news was not that the Mets lost a game to anyone in 1964; they did that pretty regularly in those days. In those days, according to broadcaster Lindsey Nelson, the Mets "looked like the Light Brigade at Balaclava. They bravely took the field each day and were systematically destroyed." The news, evidently, was that they had manged to lose a ball game in a place where no one had even played one before.

The most significant April 17 in baseball, as far as I am concerned, was this past one. I was given four season tickets to the Sounds games for my birthday. It was a milestone for me; I never had season tickets to a ballpark before. It is easily the best birthday present that I have ever received.

BACK IN THE THIRD INNING, LAKER, THE CATCHER for the home team, had turned a fastball into a home run in about a second and a half. On its way out of the park it passed one of my son's personal Greer Stadium historical markers. It was the ball that caromed off the pole, the one that took a hard left turn down past the left-field bullpen, down into the picnic areas that are set up with tents and tables. Down into Leon Durham Alley. At least that is what I and my kids call it.

Leon Durham played for the Chicago Cubs years ago. "Back in the day," as my children say, and say often these days while I am remembering old stories and telling them around the table. He played in the outfield some, and then later he played first base, I think. It was during the eighties that I watched him, during the time that I lived in Chicago, so I remembered him immediately the day that my kids and I saw him at Greer Stadium.

We had gone to the ballpark early, hoping to catch a little batting practice and find a baseball or two that had been hit over the fence. There are hitting cages that stay up all of the time down below the left-field stands, and sometimes you can see someone hitting off a tee, just as they do in tee-ball, trying to groove their swing or work out a kink in it or some such thing. Sometimes, there will be a hitter and a few feet away there will be somebody tossing balls up softly so that the hitter can practice his swing by slamming balls into a net. We were wandering back there to see what there was to see and suddenly what there was to see was Leon Durham.

He stopped playing years ago, but has found his way into a job as a hitting instructor for the Cubs' farm team in Iowa. On this afternoon, he was sitting on a stool, tossing up balls from the bucket at his feet so that a prospect for the Cubs could take extra swings and work on his hitting stroke. We stood and watched for a few minutes. He would toss a ball, the kid would pound it into the net, and Durham would say something quietly to him. Then another ball, another swing, another mumble. It was mesmerizing, in some odd sort of way. It is the same drill that we do together at the ballpark, the kids and I, and I think it tickled them to watch a professional ballplayer have to do the same thing. It made me look like a pretty smart coach, if you ask me.

A ball missed the net and then just barely missed Leon and bounced off the back of the cage and then hit the bucket and rolled over and stopped right down by my daughter's feet. We looked down at it and I knew what she was thinking. I was thinking the same thing. Neither of us moved, we just kept watching Leon tossing the balls up to the young prospect. In a few minutes the bucket was empty and the hitter started to pick up the balls. As the young player got close to the ball at her feet, Leon looked at my daughter and grinned and nodded and mumbled and the young player held up the edge of the screen. My daughter stuck her hand under the net and scooped up the ball. The three of us walked away, and as we did, she held up the baseball proudly.

"Do you know who that was?" I asked them as we walked along. I was going for the "father tells baseball story about major leaguer" move that has impressed them a couple of times in the past. "That was Leon Durham," I told them, as though they might have some clue who he was. They did not; they were not even alive when I watched him play. So I told them the story of seeing him play in Wrigley Field all those years ago. And that led to questions, and then stories about how I came to be in Chicago in the first place, and then how I came to move back home, and then how they came to be alive after all of that. It was one of those sweet moments that a father gets from time to time, when the stories that are important to him seem to be important to his children as well, and so he tells them and hopes that someday they will remember both the story and the telling of it on a late-summer afternoon with the sun going down and the green field of the game at their feet.

We pressed on to our seats, and then the kids started running around here and there doing all of the things that kids do at the ballpark before the game starts. They went to visit the booth set up out past the right-field stands where you can pay a quarter and fire a few pitches that are measured by the speed gun that tells you how fast you threw the ball. They went to see the lemonade guy, the one with the big straw hat. More and more, as my kids get older, they run into friends there too, and this time they saw some of them and cruised the stands for a bit. We have moved closer to the ballpark now, and they see friends from school nearly every time that they go. They are old hands at the ballpark by now and usually their friends are happy to hook up with them because they know where to find baseballs left over from batting practice, the ones that were hit out over the fence and have not yet been retrieved. They know the best places to stand to get autographs and the right things to say to get a player's attention. They also know which concession stand sells the foot-long chili cheese dogs.

They know the ballpark pretty well, but not just because we take them there to watch other people play. They have both played ball here.

If Laker's home run had stayed straight, it would have gone over the wall at roughly the same spot that I once found my son sitting on top of the outfield wall at Greer Stadium. Which was no mean trick considering the fact that there are no seats out there.

A couple of summers ago, I was listening to the radio and heard an interview with the baseball coach from one of the local colleges. He was promoting a baseball camp that he and his staff were going to hold at Greer Stadium a little later in the month. When I got home, I called him, and sure enough there was still room for the kids to get in, and so I signed them up.

Every day for a week they got to go to the ballpark, lace up their cleats in the dugout, hit in the cages, chase fly balls across that beautiful green stretch of grass, and generally walk around pretending that they were actual major leaguers. The fact that it was a minor league park and that it was only summer camp did not bother them a bit.

I was green with envy the whole time. I would have paid double the fee to get to go down there with them. They both had a pretty good week at camp too. My daughter, who goes by a nickname that you could use for your son if you wanted to, sort of surprised the coaching staff when she showed up because *she* showed up. They were expecting two boys named Benson, and generally speaking, not a lot of girls had showed up for baseball camp. In fact, she was the only high-school-age girl who did. They were impressed that she would even show up, and then they were even more impressed when it turned out that she could play the game. One of the coaches was the hitting instructor for the girls' softball team at the college, and he started talking to her about what it would take to make a college team about twenty minutes after her first turn in the cage.

My son worked out the first day with the kids his age, and the second day, they moved him up to work out with high-school-age kids. He is not a big guy, chip off the old block and all of that, but he is fast, and quick with his hands, and he understands the game, and pretty soon he was being chosen pretty quickly for the afternoon pickup games that got played toward the end of the day when the drills were all done.

There was a pickup game going on out in center field when I arrived to take them home one day. By then, the grounds crew was busy working on the infield for that night's game, and so the campers were using the center-field wall for a backstop and hitting back toward home plate. From time to time, someone would foul the ball off and it would start toward the left-field wall but not clear it. At Greer, there is a fence that goes up about ten feet, and then there is a walkway, about three feet wide, and then another fence that goes up about ten more feet. I suspect that they use the walkway to work on the scoreboard in left field, but I do not know for sure. At any rate, when I arrived, my son was sitting cross-legged on the walkway above left field, watching the pickup game go on down below him.

At first I was worried, thinking he had been left out of the game, but when it was his turn to bat, he would come down to hit, and when it was over he would be lifted back up on the walkway to chase the foul balls. Two of the big kids would come over and lift him high up over their heads until he could grab the top of the wall, and then he would scramble up and have a seat, with his glove on, ready to make whatever plays he had to make. Foul-ball chaser is not one of the glamour positions like shortstop or pitcher, but any way to get to the big leagues will do, I suppose. Furthermore, it is one of the few positions that you can play while sitting down, which is the sort of thing that appeals to him.

ONCE LAKER'S HOME RUN HAD HIT THE FOUL POLE and bounced down into Leon's Alley, those of us who were watching the game got caught up in watching the Sounds manager and the umpire having their discussion about whether the ball was foul or fair.

But way around to our left, there was a scramble as a dozen or so kids went flying down the stairs to try to find the ball. Who cares if it was fair or foul? There was a free baseball at stake here, a baseball with a mark on it from a professional ballplayer's bat, and maybe a little dirt on it too, a ball that could be put up onto a shelf next to the other treasures that you collect when you are growing up, when treasures come flying at you almost daily.

Coming home from the ballpark with a baseball is sort of the crowning achievement for any kid who goes to a ball game. Actually, now that I think of it, I have to admit that I have seen grown-ups go after a foul ball pretty hard. The other night my son came home with an even dozen.

That time, for one reason or another, just the two of us have gone to the game. Usually there are four of us who go, but it is just us this time, and we get there a little early. We have just missed batting practice, but it is still in that stretch of time just before the game when the crowd is still filing in and the grounds-keepers are raking and lining and spraying and tidying up the field. It always reminds me of the way that my mother and father used to go around the house and the yard just before company came.

When you get to the ballpark that early, you can sort of stroll your way to your seats, and talk to the ushers that you know, stop to chat up the beer man that works the section that you sit in, and put the starting lineups into your scorecard so that you are all ready to go when the umpire shouts, "Play ball!" And if you are my son, you have time to check the back fence for baseballs.

We pull into the driveway that goes around behind the fences and head toward the lower parking lot where I like to park. "Dad, wait!" my son yells, and hops out of the car, runs about two feet, and picks up two baseballs. "You watch your side, and I'll watch mine," he commands as he gets back into the car. "And go real slow." Another twenty-five feet, another three baseballs—one of which he has to lie down and reach up under a fence to get. By now he is not even bothering to get back into the car, and I am just sort of following him slowly, as though I am the support team for a man running a long-distance race. By the time we park the car, he has a half-dozen Official Pacific Coast League baseballs. And he has a grin a mile wide on his face and the beginning of a major remembrance in his memory.

He puts two of the cleanest ones in his pocket, along with the marker that he brings to the games in case he gets a ball and wants to get it signed by the guy who hit it or threw it to him. When we get to our seats, he says that he will be right back, he is just going to wander out through the section at the end of the right-field line and around behind the center-field wall to see if there are any balls out there. He is back in a few minutes with his hat in his hands, and it is full of baseballs. "Can I have the car key? I can't hold all these for the whole game," he says. Now we are up to a dozen and they have not even announced the starting lineup.

He comes back in a few minutes, grinning. "I found another one on the way back from the car," he reports, and settles into his seat to watch the ceremonial first pitch being thrown out. It has been a good night for him already.

On this evening, there are three ceremonial first pitches, and after one of them, the catcher turns and flips the ball into the stands, and of course he flips it to my son, who happens to be the closest kid. Then my son gets the ball autographed by the man who throws out the last of the ceremonial first pitches, Tommy Lasorda, the Hall of Fame Dodger manager who is in town to see the game because the visitors are a Dodgers farm team and he still does some scouting and such for the Dodgers even though he retired from managing some years ago.

There is now this moment frozen in my memory: my son sitting cross-legged on top of the visitors' dugout, with the last bits of sunlight behind him out in left field, with the green of the grass and the red of the infield mingled with the glow of the sun, and a Hall of Famer signing a clean white baseball and talking to my boy and both of them grinning at the sheer joy and comfort of all of this. Later in the evening, my son turns to me and confirms what I had thought to myself as I watched him sitting on top of the dugout. About the seventh inning, my son, who is thirteen now, and seldom does so anymore, crawls up into my lap, and says, "Dad, I think this our best trip to the ballpark ever."

I DO NOT KNOW IF MY CHILDREN WILL REMEMBER any of these things when they are grown-ups and taking their kids to the ballpark. I do not even know for sure that they will take their kids to the ballpark, though Heaven knows that I have tried to be a good parent. If they learn to be responsible adults, pay their taxes, stay out of jail, hold a good job and do good work, be kind to their neighbors and clean their rooms and vote in local and national elections, but do not take their kids to the ballpark, I will have failed them somehow.

I do not know if they will remember the tarp being pulled up during the rain delays, or the clubhouse guy who came out that night in the rain and slid in the puddles, making us all laugh and cheer even though we were cold and wet and shivering. I do not know if they will keep the baseballs or remember sitting on the left-field fence or in the dugouts.

There is no way to tell if they will remember the day that we went to the game and looked at our ticket stubs and discovered that their faces were on the tickets, because the team photographer had taken their picture the summer before and then used it when they printed tickets for the next season. I do not know how long my son will remember the picnic on the stone wall or how long my daughter will remember hitting in the cage where the big guys hit.

One cannot know if my kids will remember meeting Lasorda or Durham or any of the others. Or watching Nunez as he would fly down the base paths or Wehner diving behind second base to rob somebody of a hit or Laker hitting one over the wall as though it was so easy that anyone could do it. Or even if it will matter much to them if they do.

Will they remember checking on Nunez's stats that summer at the beach? Will they remember keeping score next to me in the stands? Will they take their kids to hit baseballs in the spring? I do not know the answers to those questions either.

"What I do know," wrote Roger Angell once when he was trying to sum up his feelings about the game and the people who love it, "is that this belonging and caring is what our games are all about; this is what we come for." True enough, I think.

I do not know if my kids will remember any of these things, or if they do that they will hold them to be as dear as I do. But from time to time I have a sneaking suspicion, a suspicion that is the beginning of a hope, that they will remember.

MORE THAN ANYTHING, WHAT I HOPE THEY WILL REmember are the things that the game can teach them.

I hope that they will remember that baseball is a game about going home. And in that way at least, it is a game that mirrors everything, because everything in life is about going home again. It is about leaving home, and going out to a place where home is far away, and then doing the things that you must to get home again, some of them simple and routine, some of them occasionally heroic and glorious.

I hope that they will remember that the only thing worth doing is the thing that you love to do and have been given the gifts to do and have found a place in which to do it, whether it be playing a game on a green field in the sun, or teaching a child to read in a classroom in a school, or writing a sentence in a room where no one visits. And that they will recall from time to time that the game that has called them, be it baseball or biology or bus driving, requires that they learn the steps in its dance and practice them well. That only then can they hope to do it with the joy and the grace that it deserves.

I wish for them that they will remember that there will be days when the best that can be done is to move the runner, and to offer themselves up for someone else; that what happens to them is not as important as what they can do for someone else. I wish, too, for them to remember that even the best of us, and not just the worst of us, strike out a fair amount, and come home at the end of the day with not much to show for our efforts. That life is like that somehow, a series of routine plays and sacrifices and near misses that are part and parcel of life itself.

If I could decide, then I would have them remember, too, that there will be days in their life when they will be the star, the center of some universe, large or small. Days when they will be the one who hit the ball out of the park somehow and those around them will cheer loud and long. I hope that they remember that such times are precious and fleeting and glorious, and not to be missed because one is not paying attention.

And I hope that they will remember that there are other days as well, days when their hearts will be broken, when the home team will come up empty, and that there will be little cause for joy in Mudville or anywhere else. And that on those days they can stand up and sing as well, perhaps even more than once, for it is often the only thing left for any of us to do.

In the end, I hope that they will remember some of these stories and add to them their own. I want them to remember the days when we sat in the sunshine, when we were young and strong, and the call to play ball was the best sound on earth.

MY SNEAKING SUSPICION THAT THEY WILL REMEM-ber began when my daughter left our seats at the ballpark the night that we saw Leon, saying that she would be right back. She and her brother were whispering between them for a minute or two, and then she went off up the stairs. She was gone for a while, and though I was not worried about whether or not she would be okay, I was anxious for her to get back for the start of the game. She has started keeping score along with me now, and it makes her a little crazy to miss anything.

In a few minutes she slipped in beside me just as the national anthem was over and the crowd shouted, "Play ball." She tapped me on the arm and held out a baseball. It had Leon's signature on it.

"It's for you, Dad. For bringing us to the ballpark."

AFTERWORD AND
NOTES AND SUCH

A. BARTLETT GIAMATTI

was at various times a teacher of the classics, the president of Yale, the Commissioner of Major League Baseball, and, in my opinion, one of the finest writers to ever write about the game. In 1998, a few years after his death, Algonquin Books of Chapel Hill published a collection of some of his best baseball writings in a book called *A Great and Glorious Game*. All of us who love the game and have had a chance to read his work are grateful to Algonquin for making the work available to us. If you love the game and do not have a copy, I suggest you find one as soon as you can.

There are some other books that I kept by my side as I wrote my own, partly because they are some of my favorites, and partly because they are rich sources of quotes and stories and anecdotes.

Paul Dickson's *Baseball's Greatest Quotations* (HarperCollins, New York, 1991) is as complete as any such book that I have ever seen, and was invaluable to me. Another of his books, *The Joy of*

Keeping Score (Walker & Company, New York, 1996), is a treasure as well and I recommend it to anyone who wants to learn to keep score or wants to learn to have more fun while doing so. George Gibson himself gave it to me one day at a book show, good baseball man and friend that he is to me, and I am glad to have it.

I also recommend George Will's *Men at Work* (Macmillan Publishing Company, New York, 1990). It is perhaps one of the two or three best baseball books ever written.

No one makes a book, be it about baseball or anything else, without the help of others, and I never finish one without wanting to say thank you, and to say that I could not have done this alone.

I owe a great deal to the management, the staff, and the players who make up Nashville Sounds Baseball here in my hometown. None of them knew that I was writing about them, so what I am grateful for is not their help in specific but rather their kindness and graciousness in general. Their ballpark is a fine place to go and watch a ballgame, and to spend an evening with my friends and my family. Whatever errors or misinformation appear here in regard to them is my own fault and not theirs. And furthermore, should I have inadvertently written anything that gives offense to any one of them, I plead clumsiness. I hope they can tell by the work that I am a fan of the game and of the Sounds and that I mean no disrespect to either.

There are some people, though, who helped with this book in very specific ways: Joel Fotinos and Denise Silvestro, who offered me the chance to make this book; Ken Siman, Lori Fuller, and

Phyllis Grann, who said the right words of encouragement to me along the way at times when I needed it; and Sara Carder, who inherited the work and this writer and did so with generosity and hospitality—the people at Tarcher/Putnam are always kind and gracious to me when I am trying to write, and I am always humbled and grateful.

Thank you as well to Cindy Dupree and to Bo Siler, without whose help I can never begin a book at all.

And finally to #9, my resident middle infielder, the Grillmeister, my resident humorist, and Ms. Jones of Merigold, my resident best friend on the planet—thank you, again. No finer companions are to be found.

The Author

ABOUT THE AUTHOR

Robert Benson has spent his whole life publishing, editing, writing, and otherwise wrestling with words on paper. In addition to his writing, he frequently speaks at retreats, workshops, and conferences in the areas of prayer and spirituality, vocation and calling, and writing and publishing.

He keeps score at baseball games, travels with his baseball glove in his suitcase, hits fungoes for anybody, anywhere, anytime, and still believes that he will one day be able to hit a curveball.

He is always happy to hear from those who are kind enough to read his work, and if you write to him at the address below, he will write you back.

CORRESPONDENCE

Robert Benson
Acklen Station
No. 128311
Nashville, TN 37212

SPEAKING ENGAGEMENTS:

McKinney & Associates,
Post Office Box 5162,
Louisville, KY 40255

They can also be reached at www.mckinneyspeakers.com.